Advance Praise for
MANHATTAN CULT STORY

"An extremely valuable, cogent addition to the cult memoir canon. Schneider pens his haunting story not only with vividness and vulnerability but also with an eye to humanizing the cult experience and helping survivors of such abuse—and all of us, really—understand behavior that seems inexplicable."—**Amanda Montell, author of** *Cultish: The Language of Fanaticism*

"Schneider delivers this scintillating story on a silver platter, offering a meticulous exploration of the seductive hook of meaning and fulfillment, which cults and demagogues so readily promise to their faithful. His book will be powerfully healing for those who have been lured, educational for those who haven't, and insightful for voyeurs into the delicious details of a secret world. *Manhattan Cult Story* is a vibrant, cohesive template of how the sticky tendrils of coercive control operate."—**Sarah Edmondson, author of** *Scarred: The True Story of How I Escaped NXIVM, the Cult That Bound My Life*

"It takes courage to share the stories of how we were dupgd, but even one voice can break the silence and expose the perpetrators. Schneider speaks out about his experiences in a manipulative and abusive cult, not hidden on some compound in Texas, but thriving among the educated elite of NYC. This sinister cult lures people with what they long for: community, belonging, higher purpose and elitism, but ultimately demands full obedience and control of their life. Think it couldn't happen to you?"—**Faith Jones, author of** *Sex Cult Nun: Breaking Away from the Children of God, A Wild, Radical Religious Cult*

"If the psychology of cults and cult leaders hold even a minor fascination, I heartily endorse Spencer Schneider's debut memoir of a little-known Manhattan underworld. As Schneider peels back the curtain, he brings the reader along on his journey of self-discovery. It's a story of friendship and connection, of brainwashing and trauma, and his attempt to make himself whole in the years since his daring exit."—**Amanda M. Fairbanks, author of** *The Lost Boys of Montauk: The True Story of the Wind Blown, Four Men Who Vanished at Sea, and the Survivors They Left Behind*

"Schneider has written a book I've long been waiting for: a lionhearted, soul-searching tale that flips the script of cult memoir, revealing that no one is immune to the siren call of belonging, and that any feet, no matter how well-shod, can stumble down the slippery slope of radicalism. *Manhattan Cult Story* is a book America desperately needs."—**Shawna Kay Rodenberg, author of** *Kin: A Memoir*

"This penetrating and often painful personal account written by a cult survivor details the inner workings of a secretive cult that preyed upon sophisticated, educated, and affluent New Yorkers. Spencer Schneider's twenty years of experience in 'The Work,' led by former actress turned philosopher queen Sharon Gans, demonstrates how anyone can be tricked and trapped by a deceptive cult, even those among us that seem too smart and accomplished to be taken in. This book is a deep dive into a hidden cult's world of sexual and financial exploitation, manipulation, isolation and personal destruction. Schneider spares no one including himself. Riveting and insightful." —**Rick Alan Ross, author of** *Cults Inside Out: How People Get In and Can Get Out*

"*Manhattan Cult Story* is one of those gripping tales of personal struggle and perseverance you simply cannot put down."—**Andy Ostroy, filmmaker, and director of HBO's** *Adrienne*

"*Manhattan Cult Story* is a study of human psychology, group behavior, adulation and domination, and about how a community that at first nourishes you can come to feed on you. It is a must read for anyone interested in cults, swindlers, and charlatans but also in the human

MANHATTAN
CULT STORY

yearning for deeper meaning, love, and community. The lessons of this astonishing book resonate long after the reading."—**Spencer Wolff, author of** *The Fire in His Wake*

"Intelligent, witty, and utterly terrifying. An intimate look at the break-down of everyday individuals through systematic methods of coercion and manipulation. Spencer's heartfelt account of his experiences shows how cults can and do exist all around us and are, unknowingly to most, made up of typical people you pass by every single day. Let Spencer's published voice be the first of many sincere survivors who come forward to shed light on this darkest of secret groups."—**Kacey, Host of** *The Cult Vault Podcast*

"No genre is more popular today than true-crime, and nonfiction sto-ries about cults, from NXIVM to Rajneeshism, captivate us with a par-ticular intensity. But what Schneider has done is different, and probably without parallel: He has written a highly intelligent, highly detailed, and extraordinarily compelling account from a follower's perspective. With dispassionate clarity, he takes the reader by the hand and leads them step by step down the ladder of his own subjugation. This book is an act of great bravery, and students of the cult experience owe him a debt of gratitude for it."—**Bess Rattray, publisher** *EAST Magazine*

"Written with candor, self-knowledge, and good humor, this account of Spencer Schneider's long captivity by a group of pseudo-mystic predators is first a reminder of the perils of surrendering your skep-ticism and finally a tale of self-liberation from the illusions any of us might create. *Manhattan Cult Story* pulled me in and threw away the key."—**Mike DeCapite, author of** *Jacket Weather*

"This is a gripping story about being pulled into a cult that was masked as an enrichment course, and a heartbreaking tale of manipulation, power, and greed. Spencer Schneider's well-crafted narrative is master-fully told through the lens of time, healing, and introspection. I couldn't get enough!"—**Frances Badalamenti, author of the novels** *I Don't Blame You* **and** *Salad Days*

MANHATTAN CULT STORY

MY UNBELIEVABLE TRUE STORY OF SEX, CRIMES, CHAOS, AND SURVIVAL

SPENCER SCHNEIDER

Arcade Publishing • New York

Arcade Publishing books may be purchased in bulk at special discounts
for sales promotion, corporate gifts, fund-raising, or educational purposes.
Special editions can also be created to specifications. For details, contact the Special Sales
Department, Arcade Publishing, 307 West 36th Street, 11th Floor, New York,
NY 10018 or arcade@skyhorsepublishing.com.

Arcade Publishing® is a registered trademark of Skyhorse Publishing,
Inc.®, a Delaware corporation.

Visit our website at www.arcadepub.com.

10 9 8 7 6 5 4 3 2 1

Library of Congress Cataloging-in-Publication Data is available on file.

Cover design by Erin Seaward-Hiatt

ISBN: 978-1-950994-55-7
Ebook ISBN: 978-1-950994-57-1

Printed in the United States of America

For my parents, my brother, and my son.

Reality exists in the human mind, and nowhere else. Not in the individual mind, which can make mistakes, and in any case soon perishes: only in the mind of the Party, which is collective and immortal. Whatever the Party holds to be the truth, is truth. It is impossible to see reality except by looking through the eyes of the Party.

George Orwell, *1984*

[This film] is wholly concerned with the obvious endeavors of a husband to drive his wife slowly mad. And with Mr. Boyer doing the driving in his best dead-pan hypnotic style, while the flames flicker strangely in the gas-jets and the mood music bongs with heavy threats, it is no wonder that Miss Bergman goes to pieces in a most distressing way.

Bosely Crowther, film review of *Gaslight*,
The New York Times, May 5, 1944

Contents

Author's Note

The events in this book are true. The characters in this book are based on real people but most of their identities have been disguised. Notable exceptions are certain leaders of School: Sharon Gans, Alex Horn, Fred Mindel, and Robert Klein.

To disguise people's identities, I have changed names, physical descriptions, and occupations. In some instances, other identifying traits (such as backgrounds) have been altered. I have also created a handful of composite characters based on actual people and events. Finally, in some instances, I have distorted or omitted certain immaterial surrounding events.

Preface

We were invisible. We had to be. We took an oath of absolute secrecy. We never even told our families who we really were. We thought nothing of lying. We understood that disclosure would put in us grave danger. But we liked it this way.

So we went about our lives. We worked in midtown or on Wall Street, bought our groceries at Citarella, dined out at the Odeon, spent weekends in the Hamptons, and took the subway home to comfortable apartments across the city where we lived lives of quiet privilege. We were just like you. We were your accountants, money managers, lawyers, executive recruiters, general contractors, doctors. We went to college and graduate school with you in Cambridge or Princeton or New Haven. We owned your child's private school and sold you your brownstone. But you'd never guess our secret lives, how we lived in silent terror and fervor and suffering. There were several hundreds of us.

We had our own language. We spoke in code. We covered our study books. We kept no notes. We didn't know one another's phone numbers, but we were as thick as thieves—closer than family—"essential friends." We disdained "sleeping humanity," and strove to be "awake." We had a sophisticated system to unsuspectingly befriend, vet, and recruit you—in the subway, at Bloomingdale's, the neighborhood bookstore, Lincoln Center, Starbucks, Nobu. We were students of an esoteric school—we called it "School." Even if you somehow knew about us, you would never be able to find us.

We met for class two nights a week at "the Space," an unfinished, white-walled, open loft over a nondescript wholesale fabric store on a deserted stretch of Broadway below Canal Street. Our tallest man stood guard downstairs, alone, in blizzards and choking heat, to let us in, one by one, nodding, silently opening the rickety gray steel door with the cracked chicken wire windowpane. The dark hallway's faded paint was peeling, the rusty tin ceiling was disintegrating, and it smelled of clove and cardamom from the spice factory over on Franklin Street. Alone, we arrived promptly at 7:00 p.m., left well after midnight, and kept our "hour of silence." There was no signage. No chatter. The intercom was broken. We were saving civilization; we were gaining ancient knowledge to obtain our "perfection."

We revered our teacher—whose name we were forbidden to utter outside her presence—referred to simply as "S." There she was, upstairs in the Space, recumbent on her leather recliner, surrounded by sixty of us seated on white stackable metal chairs, hanging on every one of her words. S's wild mane of Halloween-orange hair hung over her flowing black dress and silk scarf. Sixty-five years old, she had deep-set cerulean eyes, pasty white skin, and a hawk-beak nose. Bedecked in jewelry, she puffed on a cigarette, her smoke filling the poorly ventilated loft. She spoke in her falsetto singsong voice, expounding at length about placing School above all else. We weren't engrossed—we were transfixed, under her total command. We felt her brilliance, her emanations, her love (or wrath), her ferocity, her power.

You see, she possessed an ancient oral wisdom, which she maintained was directly traceable to the mystery schools and Pythagoras. Incredibly, it was available to us here in Manhattan in 1992. It was called the "Work." She taught us how to achieve "higher mind" and ignore "false morality." And we feared her—as if she could destroy us, at her whim.

For S we would do anything. She gave us detailed directions on how to live our lives. She regulated everything. This was all for our evolution. Where to work. Who of our classmates to sleep with, marry, divorce. What to think. What scientific truths should be disbelieved. What social conventions should be ignored. Whether someone's child should be given up for adoption to other students. Whether a gay male student should be married off to a female student in order to be "straightened out." Whether to cut off relationships with family and friends. She instructed some of us to cheat on our spouses and sleep with other students. She married off some of us to complete strangers. She had us labor on huge construction projects for free. Some were privileged to help her launder cash and commit tax fraud. We would do anything for her. Some would have gone to jail or killed for S, our teacher, Sharon Gans.

This was long ago. We were so young. We were hungry for meaning, friends, knowledge, community, answers, support, and a paradigm to help navigate our lives. All of this—even a sense of magic—were what kept us coming back for more. We believed we were gaining unique tools to improve ourselves, and so we granted Sharon full access into our hearts, conscience, bodies, and minds. But as much as we kept School secret from—and lied to—our families and friends, Sharon kept her secrets from us. And she lied, about everything: her checkered past, her intentions, her criminality, her substance abuse, her mental disease, her need for power and adulation, her greed, and her perversions. It was only later—after we were hooked, and it was too late—that we found out. And so, we endured (and witnessed) mental, sexual, and physical abuse, forced labor, swindling of our money, breaking up of our families, and systematic terrorizing. Some students conspired with her to break the law. Sharon left her students in shambles: poorer, broken down, beaten up, and hollowed out. Only a handful of us have ever spoken out about Sharon, privately or publicly.

During those years, I had nothing else but School—it was my world.

This is the story of how I got entangled in School, the twenty-three years I spent there, how I narrowly escaped, and how I've survived.

Sharon Gans, escorted into the Space by her acolytes. Circa 2015.
Courtesy of the author.

PART 1
1960–1989

My mother and me. Circa 1971. Courtesy of the author.

There was no straight line from my happy childhood in suburban Long Island to those white stackable metal chairs on lower Broadway. There were just life's usual twists, turns, curves, circles, and then some very bad directions combined with rotten timing.

My father was born six weeks before the Wall Street crash of 1929—the seventh child of Belarusian immigrants Esther and Meyer, who spoke only Yiddish in their home. Esther was forty-five at the time, already a grandmother, and initially mistook her pregnancy for a tumor. My father was born in their tenement on the Lower East Side. In the 1930s, many landlords lured new tenants with offers of several months of free rent. Hence my grandparents, for years, moved every several months, experiencing all that New York City had to offer. After my father returned from the Korean War, he went to college and landed a job selling records. Later he went into the advertising business, where he worked for the rest of his career. My father looked so much like Jerry Lewis that he claims Dean Martin once mistook him for his old comedy partner.

My mother's father emigrated from Austria to Brooklyn in the 1900s. A ladies' shoe store salesman, he met my grandmother when she came in to shop. They married and had a son and my mother. They lived in Brownsville, one of the poorest sections of Brooklyn. Although my grandparents considered themselves modern thinking, college was out of the question for their daughter. But my mother prevailed, and she got her degree from Hunter College. She graduated, became a grade school teacher, and was introduced by another teacher to my father.

My parents moved to Midwood, Brooklyn, where I was born in 1960. We moved to Levittown, Long Island, in 1961, and my brother, Matthew, was born in 1962. Levittown in the 1960s was a perfect place to grow up. We had the Desther kids next door, the Palmieris and their ducks down the block, the fenced-in three-acre sump behind my house, the public pool three blocks away, parents who let us play outside after dinner, and the Good Humor ice cream truck every summer night. But in 1969, my parents announced that we were moving.

They bought a big old rundown house in Hewlett Bay Park, Long Island, an upscale suburb that had no sidewalks or kids out playing. They purchased the house from the estate of someone named Hiram Cosby. I overheard my parents talking about old man Cosby. He had hanged himself in his garage—now our garage. I had never heard of such a thing. I was nine. I was surrounded by death in that house. Almost every year somebody in my family died: my grandma Esther, my grandpa Sidney, Uncle Jack, Uncle Saul, Aunt Ida, my Bubby, my cousins Ruth and Susie, who were only teenagers and so beautiful, and our cats. Still, it was Cosby's death which always haunted me, loomed over my childhood. As a thirteen-year-old paperboy, I spent every predawn morning—hot, cold, slushy, or wet—standing in that dark, haunted garage wrapping the newspapers in red rubber bands and stuffing them in my bike basket. Not a morning went by that I didn't see poor Cosby hanging there. I worked quickly, hands blackened by the *Daily News* headlines and the sports page. What kind of suffering led Cosby to hang himself? Where in the garage did he do it? Was his spirit still there? Did he go to hell? Was he now at peace? Would he hurt me? Would he hang me? I convinced my father to get a better light in the garage. I also never worked there with the door shut. When my friend Kenny took his life at eighteen years old, I thought again of Cosby, and it scared me.

I recently framed an old black-and-white photograph of my parents from around 1965, taken at a business cocktail party. My father is wearing a seersucker jacket, a white shirt, a skinny black tie, and a slight grin on his face. He's crouched down, leaning against the back of the chair where my mother sits. In his left hand he's clenching a cocktail glass with his thumb, pinky, and ring finger, and a lit cigarillo is wedged between his index and middle fingers. He's wearing Buddy Holly–style eyeglasses and his short, straight black hair is parted on the side, glistening with Brylcreem. My mother's black hair is short. She is wearing pearls, fake eyelashes, and a short dark dress that reveals her shoulders; she is flashing her beautiful movie-star smile. It's a revealing image of contradictions: my folks—young, attractive, and trendy—living a certain kind of upwardly mobile life in the 1960s, and yet I wonder how they felt. If you didn't know them you might see them as confident and at ease, enjoying themselves. But I knew them. And I understood that they felt a little out of place, like miscast actors. Maybe guilty too, and worried about the "evil eye." Even much later—after years of hard work and achieving the financial stability they wanted—they sometimes suffered from insecurity, feeling like imposters, undeserving. This was a new world for them, unlike the one they grew up in. My parents knew what it was like to have nothing, no security—they survived the Great Depression and World War II—but the sixties were uncertain times, heightening their anxiety about losing everything, going back. They were also children of immigrants who had been persecuted in their native homeland. Despite their best efforts, these feelings of insecurity, guilt, anxiety, and the irrational fear of an impending catastrophe rubbed off on me and my brother.

We lived in one of the wealthiest zip codes in the United States, but, by force of my parents' habits, lived in certain ways like we were preparing for another Great Depression. For instance, my mother refused to set the thermostat above sixty-one degrees in the dead of New York winter. "Wear a sweater," she would say, handing Matthew and me a box of tissues. Summers were intolerable in the air-conditioner-less house, so when I was fourteen, I used my paper-route money to purchase a small unit for my bedroom.

But there was a flip side of it: our parents encouraged self-reliance. By the time I was eighteen, I had also worked as a babysitter, a butcher's gofer, a caddy, and a cabana boy at the Silverpoint Beach Club in Atlantic Beach. Matthew and I had to help our father with yard work, painting, and other construction and design projects that were led by my mother. She went through a rock garden phase, and I helped her retrieve rocks from roadbeds and lug them into the car. Otherwise, we were left on our own in the 1970s and could come and go as we pleased. When I was thirteen, I was allowed to take the train into Manhattan alone and, when I was seventeen, to drive into Manhattan to go to concerts and clubs. When I was fifteen, a couple of my friends and I rode our bikes a hundred miles out to Montauk to camp out for a weekend. I don't remember having a curfew.

My father was my hero and protector, but he was not one for conversations. When he finally came around to tell me about the "birds and the bees"—I must have been twelve by this time—he sat me down to ask whether I knew how babies "were made." I assured him I did, he said "good," and it was over. Intimate conversations

My parents. Circa 1965. Courtesy of the author.

took place in his car. Neither of us looked at each other, one of us (usually him) safely and determinedly in control. In the summer of 1980, I was twenty, and we were driving home from the envelope factory where he'd gotten me a summer job. "So, are you sure you want to go to law school?" he asked. I'd wanted to be a lawyer ever since I saw *To Kill a Mockingbird*. I wanted to be like Atticus Finch, fighting for justice, against all odds. I assured my father I did and told him I'd go insane if I had to work a job like customer service at the factory. He said he just wanted to be sure, that law school was expensive, but he thought he could swing it. My father never hid his worry or his pride in me. "Thanks Dad, you're the best." He patted my leg.

A few months before I graduated from law school, Matthew reached me in Manhattan with the news: our father had died that morning of a sudden heart attack at fifty-six in his office. I had feared that this day would come. It was a sense I had. I rushed back to Long Island, rudderless, destroyed, and I collapsed into that house, another death notched on its threshold. But I had no time to mourn, because I needed to graduate, take the bar exam, and get a job. My mother got me through it—pushy, determined, and supportive. She told me my father would want me to graduate on time and get on with it. I did. I graduated, but he missed out on witnessing me get my law degree and I missed out on him witnessing me get my law degree. I felt cheated.

Six months after graduating, I got hired by a well-regarded corporate litigation firm. But I found that working twelve-hour days and weekends doing grunt legal work, never going to court or taking testimony, and helping big corporations with their problems had nothing whatsoever to do with Atticus Finch.

The exciting life in Manhattan outside the office that I had expected didn't materialize. In my early to late teens and early twenties, (i.e., from 1978 through 1985) Manhattan was my playground of nightclubs, bars, and partying with my tight-knit group of friends from high school and college. By my late twenties, I felt isolated and bored. Although I lived in a one-bedroom apartment in Greenwich Village, my refrigerator held nothing but expired ketchup, a half dozen white cardboard takeout containers of stale rice, and a few bottles of Heineken. I used the cabinets to store old books and arts and crafts supplies. I missed my friends who were moving to the suburbs or just moving on; I rarely made any new ones.

In 1989, I called my old law school buddy Joel. We had played together in his blues band during law school, and he'd been asking me to join up again. "You still looking for a bass player?" I asked. "Yes. Can you get us some gigs, man?" Joel's band was called the Blue Laws. It consisted of him on lead guitar and several other musicians, all accomplished in blues, soul, and R&B. I joined, and we clicked. I started looking for gigs and found one at the North River Bar, one of the last longshoreman pubs on the Lower West Side of Manhattan.

PART 2
1989–1990

Bruce

That's where I met Bruce. It was the winter of 1989. He was standing behind the empty bar at the cavernous North River, smoking a Marlboro Light, and absorbed in a paperback wrapped in a homemade brown paper bag cover. He was in his mid-twenties, lanky, and handsome. He had a slightly androgynous look with thin lips, high cheekbones, and soft blue eyes. He seemed out of place in this joint. His thick black hair was parted on the side and almost fell over his eyes—like Bowie's *Young Americans* cover. He smelled of WASP: my opposite. He looked up from his book when he heard us loading in our amps and gear to set up for the night. He walked out from behind the bar, and said, "Hey guys, uh, Spanky told me to tell you that he doesn't want you to play until we fill up a bit." I introduced myself and we shook hands.

Joel and I sat at the bar waiting for a crowd to arrive. Bruce served us Buds and paper bowls of fresh popcorn. The North River always smelled of beer and hot popcorn. Turns out Bruce was working there on weekends because during the week he was getting his MBA at Columbia. He let on that he was from Oregon and graduated from Princeton University. Joel and I told him we were law school friends and the three of us joked about how our advanced degrees had us in the North River. The other bartender was Maxie, a young Irish woman who was loud, fun, and attractive. Over the next couple of months, I saw Bruce maybe four times, and our interactions were confined to light chitchat during breaks: the weather, the crowd, how the night was going, his tips, our cover fee.

Over time, the conversations got more interesting. We had a lot in common. He and I talked about our favorite architect (Frank Lloyd Wright) and buildings (the Parthenon, Chartres); our favorite philosophers (Plato, Sartre); our favorite artists (Rembrandt, Bellini); our favorite twentieth-century writers (Kafka, Orwell). I hadn't talked about these topics with anyone since I graduated from Washington University in 1982. And I loved it. I had missed it. He also started to ask me personal questions: why I decided to become a lawyer, whether I liked it, and how I felt working for big law. I explained how I had gone into it because I liked the idea of fighting for justice but how disappointing and disillusioning it was doing grunt work for soulless bosses and faceless corporate clients. It got so that I started to look forward to breaks for my talks with Bruce. He was interested in what I had to say, and I liked that. I didn't know details of his life, like where he lived or what his friends were like, but he was cool and smart.

But shortly thereafter, things changed: Bruce began what felt like stalking. He showed up unannounced one night in the control room at a studio in downtown Brooklyn while our band recorded a demo. He said he was curious to see the "artistic process." No idea how he knew I was there and there was no reason for him to be there. Then a week later he called me at the office—no idea how he got the number—and said he "happened to be nearby." I was not happy to hear from him—this was annoying and disruptive—but I reluctantly agreed to meet him at the Italian place downstairs on East Forty-fifth Street. We got a table outside on that hot day and he wanted to know about my upbringing, my worldviews on politics, and my personal aspirations. The easygoing chats at the bar had given way to an interrogation. Even over the din of honking cars and truck air brakes, he seemed to find this all fascinating and, despite being slightly put off by his relentlessness, I couldn't help but feel flattered, enjoying the attention. The topic finally shifted back to philosophy and art and truth and beauty and meaning. We paid the check and then it got weird again: he randomly asked whether I would "like to go on an adventure sometime?" I had no idea what he meant so I just nodded politely, and Bruce vanished into the traffic on East Forty-fifth Street.

The next afternoon I heard from Bruce again at the office. "Spencer, I have to talk to you about something," he said urgently. "Meet me tonight at 7:00 p.m. at the Cedar Tavern on University Place, OK?" he said without elaborating. I was curious and agreed. "OK, see you there," I said.

The Cedar Tavern had a rich history—in the 1950s it was frequented by writers like Jack Kerouac and Allen Ginsberg, and painters such as William de Kooning and Jackson Pollock (who was allegedly banned for tearing off and throwing the bathroom door at the painter Franz Kline).

On this warm July evening in 1989, I took the express train directly from the office where my boss had been on my back to finish writing a memo. I was still wearing my dark suit, with my Brooks Brothers tie undone, briefcase in hand. From the bright New York early summer evening, I stepped up into the Cedar Tavern and was momentarily blinded by its darkness. I squinted and scanned the nearly empty bar making out Bruce way in the back room, seated alone, with his back to me. I walked past the long mahogany bar and its ghosts—locals, barflies, beat poets, abstract expressionists, all getting drunk, laughing, crying, fighting, and puking. My shiny black business shoes plowed through the sawdust soaked in their words, paint, vomit, and blood.

By the time I approached Bruce, my pupils were fully adjusted. He was in a fresh pink Izod shirt and pressed khakis. I walked up to and around the table. He stood to shake my hand and awkwardly grinned. I sat facing him, toward the front where I could see the thin rays of sunlight spilling into the bar room through the old blinds. The Cedar's back room smelled faintly like urine, so I skipped ordering food and opted for a Heineken; he ordered a Coke and onion rings. It was claustrophobic back there, as if Bruce were somehow blocking my exit.

Bruce was tense. It was making me tense. I was wondering why I kept agreeing to one-on-one meetings with a guy I barely knew. What on earth could be so urgent?

After the waitress took our order, I asked "OK, Bruce, what's all the cloak and dagger?"

He started slowly, in a soft wavering voice, looking right at me, "There's something I need to speak with you about. It's not something I've ever told anyone."

I rolled my eyes and wondered, *why me*? I said, "It's OK. Are you about to come out to me?"

"No," he said blushing.

The waitress brought our drinks, giving us both a chance to reset, take a sip, and light up cigarettes. I looked past him, over his shoulder to the front room and the thin rays of light; Bruce's face was blurry in our smoke, and for a moment I didn't know where I was. I took a deep drag. He did too. The smoke billowed over the table, the nicotine filled my brain, relaxing me. My heartbeat accelerated with my curiosity.

Bruce shifted to a formal tone, slowly explaining, "I didn't mean to alarm you, but there's a timing issue, so I wanted to get ahold of you. It's something I deeply cherish"—*cherish?*—"and that's why I never discuss it. But I've got to ask if you can keep this between us and not talk about it with anyone?"

He waited and I shrugged. "Sure, but who would I tell?"

"Well I don't mean just Joel or the band, but anyone. It's private," he said.

By now I was dying to hear what he had to tell me. We lit up new cigarettes.

Bruce continued solemnly, choosing each word carefully, "I'm a student of a school. It's an esoteric school that is hidden, it's invisible. That's why we've got to keep this private." *I'm listening.* "These schools have existed since ancient times. Their knowledge has been passed down orally from generation to generation. Its focus is the meaning of life, how to find truth, inner freedom." He could see my face, body pulling back. He assured me, "They're not bullshit. But they aren't for everyone. It's been said that Shakespeare was in a school; even the philosophers and artists we mentioned—Plato, Rembrandt, and Frank Lloyd Wright in modern times." *This sounds even more super-duper sketchy, exciting, and dangerous.* "The school that exists in New York is the only one of its kind here and it traces its roots directly to ancient times." *It sounds like he's going to invite me.* "I'm telling you because there is an opportunity for new people to study. This opening doesn't happen much; it's closing soon." *Now this sounded rehearsed.* "It has helped me get the things I want in life. I know you want to get something out of life rather than just your work." With that, Bruce studied my face while he took a drag of his Marlboro Light, with a shaky hand. "What do you think? There's a monthlong period, an experiment, where you can come to class and try it out." He flicked the ashes in a small round ashtray.

I didn't know what to say. Besides it being vague and strange, I found it odd for Bruce to offer this to me, of all people. Didn't he want to offer this to someone he knew better? And yet I experienced a tingle: a secret ancient group here in Manhattan, in 1989? I remembered once hearing about secret societies where scholars met to debate. This sounded like some incredible exclusive club of Manhattan's intellectual elite, something I didn't want to miss. I felt honored. An amazing opportunity. I watched Bruce as he awaited my answer. About then the jukebox got louder—it was the Clash's "Magnificent Seven." My mind went elsewhere. Images of the Cedar's artists and poets and locals drinking and shouting. The long day at work. My memo was due tomorrow. I was hungry. Too much intrigue. Too much pressure. Too hinky.

I wanted to be honest and blunt. "Bruce, I'm not sure what to say to you. It just doesn't sound like something that would interest me. It actually sounds a little culty to me." As I said this, I could feel myself getting annoyed—angry even—because part of me felt that Bruce might have been trying to pull one over on me. Bruce took a quick drag and said nothing, looked down, blew smoke out from the side of his mouth. This was awkward. It was also disappointing—maybe I'd been hoping for him to tell me something simple, like Maxie from the bar had a crush on me. Poor Bruce was crestfallen. The meeting was over. There wasn't much to say. I shook his hand, took out ten dollars from my wallet, and I told him I had to get home.

As soon as my shoes hit the bright sidewalk of University Place outside the Cedar, I replayed in my mind what had just happened. I felt guilty. Bruce had just poured his heart out to me and I called his cherished school culty. Was I overreacting? What evidence did I have that this was a cult? None. He was a nice dude. I was being a dick. I upset him. When I got home, I called him. "I'm sorry Bruce, I didn't mean to insult you and what you are doing. Can we try this again?" I asked to meet him in Washington Square Park later.

We strolled up University Place. It was less tense walking than facing off in the smelly, empty Cedar. Dusk was approaching, and the city was vibrant and alive and filled with bus fumes and pizza parlors and traffic lights and newspaper stands selling magazines. Cars honked, a boom box blared Public Enemy's "Fight the Power." I didn't feel trapped. Bruce shouted to be heard over the bus. He said innocently, "It just seems to me that you're looking for more meaningful things to do in life and to try something new. I sensed you're maybe at a crossroads in your life. Like I said, some of the philosophers we talked about were connected to esoteric schools. Spencer, the teaching is practical, and it's an opportunity. I think you will like it. Also, the other students in the class are people like yourself—intelligent and thoughtful." And he asked rhetorically, "Do you really think that somebody like me would be in a cult?" I asked him what this group was called and he told me, "It's just called 'School.'"

Standing at the corner of University Place and East Eighth Street, I was transported to 1971, when my father took the family into the city for a field trip to explore Greenwich Village. He bought me a blacklight velvet "Peace" poster. I was awed by that magical street of color, motion, hippies, Electric Ladyland studio, and the smell of incense from the head shops. Now, here in 1989, and unable to hide my wonder at possibly happening upon something truly magical—nothing I was consciously looking for—I asked, "Such a thing operates here in Manhattan, today?" I was taking the bait. He nodded solemnly. "Take me to your leader," I joked.

He chuckled and said he wanted me to meet another student. Then he reminded me, "You remember you have to keep this strictly confidential, right?"

I said, "No problem, Bruce," as I shook his hand and we parted ways and I went home.

Heather

The next evening Bruce and I were seated at a square table overlooking East Sixteenth Street at the busy, trendy restaurant, the Blue Water Café on Union Square West. The airy room——it used to be a bank—echoed the Replacements' "I'll Be You" over the sound system, and I smelled the tuna grilling in the open-air kitchen. The room was bathed in an orange hue punctuated by the small candles at each table. I was relieved that Bruce had suggested this upscale place over another depressing tavern—it reflected better on his tastes and possibly of his "School." We smoked our cigarettes, making small talk about the North River. I asked about Maxie the bartender and whether he thought she might go out with me. I was nervous to meet his "friend," whom, he told me (upon my insistence), was an investment banker who had gone to Wharton.

And then a smiling woman in a dark gray business dress and carrying a briefcase approached our table, and tapped Bruce on his shoulder. He turned around and jumped up to embrace her. Heather was in her early thirties, with high cheekbones and blue eyes. She wore simple diamond studs and no makeup.

She sat directly across from me. As soon as the waiter took our drink orders Heather got right to business. Smiling, she said, "So, Spencer, Bruce tells me you're interested in hearing more about

School." I told her I was. Bruce and Heather smiled and she nodded, saying she would be happy to tell me more.

But first she asked me to tell her about music and how it fed my professional life. I said that I never thought of it that way, but she could have asked me anything about myself: I was just flattered by her interest in me. Heather was friendly, but she was also formal and unusually direct. Her professional demeaner brought credibility—even cachet—to Bruce's invitation. There was nothing heavy or weird or pushy about Heather. She was easygoing, authentic, and I was eager to see where this was going. She said, "I should tell you that Bruce spoke highly of you and that he wanted to extend this invitation specifically to you." The waiter delivered our drinks.

She said, "School is a special place for me, as it is for Bruce and all of the students. Like any school, there are teachers and students. But it's unlike schools which exist in 'life'—in an esoteric school, the purpose is to apply the practical knowledge you learn to your life so you can evolve. It's a school for your inner development— to perfect yourself." Heather paused, and got emotional, "It's a profound experience and it's mysterious and it's wonderful and wondrous. To change yourself is like nothing else. To find truth and freedom is sublime." I glanced at Bruce, who was also getting into an emotional state as he listened to her. I felt that I was witnessing something intimate—and I didn't understand what—but I sensed their connection, their devotion to something profound. Heather continued, "For me, I have been able to tap into parts of myself which I never knew existed and to connect with people in a new way. With the tools provided by the teachings, I have been able to get what I want." I had never heard a contemporary—or really anyone—speak like this, with this kind of serious, sincere reverence. It was still vague, but it was seductive. It sounded a little dangerous and fun. It was beguiling that a beautiful investment banker was in an esoteric school and interested in questioning the meaning of life, and that I was being invited, too.

The tables near us were filling up with smart-looking couples on dates, and I noted that the sound system was playing that same

Clash song again with that complicated bass line played by Norman Watt-Roy.

Heather asked if the offer interested me. I told her it did. She explained that School met two evenings a week to discuss the ideas of the philosopher George Gurdjieff—someone I had ever heard of despite my philosophy degree—but that for the most part it was an "oral tradition handed down through the ages."[1] She said that if I wanted to try the experiment I needed to commit to come for four weeks of classes so that I could get a sense of it because it wasn't something I could decide in just a few classes. She said that the first month's experiment was free but that after that, it would cost $300 per month. She pointed out that School is "not for everyone" and that the one-month experiment allowed "both sides to see if it's a good fit." She said, "Spencer, what would you like to work on in School in terms of yourself?"

Now I found myself in the position of wanting to impress these people. And I couldn't get over how pretty her eyes were, and she was leaning in closely. She wore a familiar musky perfume that reminded me of what my friend Vicki from high school wore. I looked at both Heather and Bruce carefully and they seemed open, and sincerely interested in what I had to say. I didn't want to blow this. I thought a bit and it just came out: "I want to be able to control myself—my thoughts and my feelings." There was a pause. They nodded in recognition, solemn, serious, satisfied. I had answered correctly.

Heather and Bruce listened to me so intently. In my life, who had listened like this? Who was *this* interested in what I had to say? Who talked about such weighty, important things? Heather responded like a close—but long-lost—friend; a kindred spirit, and we were being

---

1   I was curious. There was no Google in 1989, but I did have access to LexisNexis at my law firm. The next morning at work I looked up "Gurdjieff & New York City" and came across a Sam Shepard interview where he talked about performing in his early career for "some Gurdjieff Fourth Way School" on the Lower East Side. LexisNexis was expensive, so I signed off before coming across Gurdjieff's obituary in the October 31, 1949, edition of the *New York Times* titled, "G. I. Gurdjieff, 83, Founder of Cult; Rites Today for Mystic Whose Devotees Found Calm Through Exercises—Died in Paris."

reunited. I had the curious feeling that I had met her before. A wave of goodwill and kindness swept over me. It was like I had just been given nitrous oxide and not only could I feel no pain but every-thing—everything—was wonderful and beautiful. What had sounded suspicious now sounded mysterious and sexy even. Maybe it was like Plato's Retreat with conversations about the meaning of life? I had fully shifted. I wanted this.

Heather smiled and said, "This is great, Spencer. In School you will get a lot of material on self-mastery; it's one of the main things we study there."

Then I said I had one more question. "Who exactly teaches the classes?"

She smiled, "Teachers in esoteric schools are the oldest students, students who have traveled the path and have the knowledge to pass on."

And then this happened—a moment that seared into me: Before she continued her answer, Heather looked directly at Bruce who looked back at her with a smile, and she said to him, "Bruce, don't you think that the teachers are amazing people?" There was another pause as they both smiled at each other as though they possessed a secret that maybe—hopefully—they would let me in on. I hate/love secrets and they seemed to have an incredible one. Bruce nodded and answered, "Heather, they really are. They are rare and exceptional."

The moment was interrupted by the waiter who asked if we wanted another round. Heather and Bruce looked at their watches, said they needed to run, and asked him for the check. As they stood, Heather said that I should think about it before deciding and then let Bruce know in the next couple of days whether I wanted to come. She said, "It was so wonderful to meet you, Spencer, and I hope to see you again. I'm excited for you to take this step." And with that, they both left some cash on the table and quickly walked out together before the bill came. They hadn't quite left enough to cover their share.

The following day was like any other day: throw on blue business suit, lace up black shoes, grab cinnamon raisin bagel with plain cream cheese and chocolate milk, the hot 4 train uptown, write up memo for boss, sandwich, finish memo, dinner at desk, partners leave, coast clear, the infernal 4 train downtown. That night, I took off my suit and headed out to our hangout at Van Dams on Varick Street to meet my high school friends David, Colin, Scott, Brian, Vicki, and Nancy for drinks. They'd invited college friends to join us.

At the bar, I observed the busy bartender, my friends, their friends. I smelled the cigarette smoke, and all the perfumes, bodies, and aromas of a New York City summer night. I heard the sound system playing James Brown's "Funky Drummer." I thought of the secret Bruce and Heather shared. Not a single person here knew about it. Was their secret for real, though? I thought of Bruce and Heather's knowing glances. I wondered about the other students and the teachers they admired. I thought about how they'd left together. I fished out a quarter. I somehow remembered Bruce's number and called him from the pay phone in the back and got his machine. "Bruce, it's Spencer. I've thought about it. I'll check it out. Give me a call when you can."

Back at the bar, I felt disconnected from my old friends. I bought another vodka and cranberry juice. The scene bored me. I downed my drink, said farewell, and headed out; I caught a cab. I rolled down the window and looked out at that quiet stretch on 6th Avenue below Houston, as we passed Souen, the macrobiotic restaurant on the corner of Prince Street. It triggered memories of lunches during law school with my father. It was a mystery to me why he loved it. "Dad, the food has no taste there, can we just go to Katz's Deli?" I pleaded. "No, but you can ask for some mustard on the side," he quipped. I never could stand that place.

First Class

"Hi Spencer, it's Bruce. Meet me tomorrow night at 6:45. Corner of Canal and Broadway. Have a great day." That was the voice mail I got the next morning. On the edge of Chinatown, on that hot night, the humid air was heavy with the smell of baking garbage. The old Mudd Club was nearby, a joint where the doorman's decision to admit was a referendum on your hipness. I batted about .333 there (and the same at Studio 54). "I hope this isn't going to be weird," I said to Bruce, oblivious to the irony that this couldn't be any weirder. He told me I would have to take off my shoes at the door. I was wearing fluorescent rainbow tube socks and wondered aloud that I would look "nuts." He smirked. I had no precedent for something like this except for playing secret agent man when I was seven. Yet here I was being led—virtually blindfolded—by a virtual stranger to an undisclosed location in a smelly part of town to an "experiment" with a secret, possibly sketchy, group.

We stopped in front of a wholesale fabric store on the ground floor of a two-story loft building on Broadway and Franklin—one of those places that sells ornamental scarves and pink plaid chiffon by the yard—its moon gates down for the night. *An ancient school related to Shakespeare above a schmatte store?* We got into a moldy antique elevator. It had a creaky metal gate that closed behind us and was operated by a crank. *A crank.* It took about two minutes to make it to the second floor. We emerged into a rectangular loft with a wood floor, bare white walls, and high ceilings. Milling about were about five dozen people about my age, half of them women.

There were about sixty or so white stackable metal chairs—the kind that tend to squeak loudly when someone shifts their weight—arranged on top of sturdy unpainted wooden bleachers. At the front of the room sat two empty black director chairs, each with a small cherrywood side table upon which were placed vases of cut flowers. The room smelled of fresh paint, clean and anonymous, and coffee brewing in the urns sat on a counter in the back. The tan curtains were drawn. The place seemed generic, not at all weird. I was glad there was nobody in black robes chanting, but by the same token, I was almost disappointed. It didn't look like an underground movement or a secret society that could trace its lineage to the designers of Chartres as alleged by Bruce. Just a lot of white people. Professional. Comfortable. Nice looking. But there was nothing particularly notable about any of them. They looked, I realized, a lot like me.

After a few minutes, a woman who looked to be in her late thirties, with long dark hair and a warm smile, entered the room and approached us. Bruce introduced me to Hazel Ford, who was the owner of a successful Manhattan brokerage firm. Her voice was firm and friendly, and she had a nervous tic of blowing her hair off her face. Her lips were chapped. She wore a fragrance that immediately reminded me of the head shop I used to go to when I was fourteen to buy posters and incense. She also reminded me of my hippie older cousins.

"I'm so happy for you that you are here, Spencer. I hope this is a rich and wonderful experience for you and I think it will be," she beamed as she shook my hand. Her warmth and candor, her vibe, was like Heather's.

"Thank you, Hazel," I said, "I hope it is."

And then something notable happened—unexpected but welcome. Hazel moved her face closer to me and lowered her voice, as if to confide something, "You know, Spencer, many of us have found our soul mates here. I hope that for you too."

A man with a large frame and big smile approached us; Hazel switched gears, "Spencer, please meet Simon. He'll be holding an orientation for the new students who are starting their experiment tonight." I was ushered into a small room with a dozen other newbies. I bid farewell to Bruce. (I didn't hear from Bruce again by phone, although we continued to see each other at the North River.)

Simon asked us to sit on the floor in a circle and introduce ourselves. Simon was well over six feet, with what seemed like a slight hunchback; he favored corduroys and cardigans with patches (even in July) and was a successful, brilliant painter by profession. His voice was deep and soothing, like a pilot on a transatlantic flight, confident and reassuring. "Welcome to your experiment, I'm so happy for you to be here. I hope you find this meaningful and special." Before we went into class, Simon ran through some guidelines and rules intended, he assured us, to enhance our experiment and to help us practice the principles of the Work. These same rules, we were told, have applied to all esoteric schools throughout the ages. They were for our benefit—to help us evolve.

He continued, in his composed manner, "The first and most important rule is invisibility. Esoteric schools are hidden and invisible by their nature. For the knowledge to be protected, it must remain invisible. You should not discuss the ideas or knowledge outside of class with anyone. You should not even talk about the existence of School with anyone. It would be a 'leak'—it drains your energy, an idea you will learn about later in your month's experiment. Invisibility is for your own benefit. And it is also essential for the protection of School and for everyone who attends. A leak can destroy School, can make it disappear, and once it's gone it is gone. So, if anyone asks where you are going on class nights you can tell them that it's private and say no more." This was all fine by me: I didn't want to have to explain anything to anyone about this experiment. I preferred to have a secret.

"There is a rule against fraternizing with other students outside of class," Simon said. "No phone numbers are to be exchanged. There is an hour of silence to maintain immediately after class ends—use it to reflect on class and let the knowledge sink in. Also, when you leave here after class, you are to go your separate ways—do not share cabs or take the train together. It goes without saying that you cannot meet with each other outside of class. If you coincidentally bump into each other on the street or subway or anywhere, just look the other way and carry on. Say hello in your heart. It's very important for you and for School to maintain invisibility. This is how you will create 'Essence Friendships.' 'Essence' is the deepest part of a being and friendships connected by Essence are like no others—they are profound, interconnected, and the dearest relations one can have. They are distinguished from 'life' friendships. Essence friendships are based entirely on helping others achieve their 'Aims' of consciousness, whereas 'life' friendships tend to be superficial and based upon enabling each other's weaknesses." I couldn't square this with what Hazel had just confided with me about soul mates or the special bond Heather and Bruce seemed to have.

Classes started at seven, and Simon told us we had to arrive ten minutes early. He said we needed to "leave our days at the door." Each class would begin with twenty minutes of "body work"—light move-ment exercises designed to help "loosen your body." On alternate nights we would learn and practice the tai chi movements. Classes were to last until midnight, although sometimes they could run later.

He added there was to be no drug use, as it was "detrimental to evolution." This wasn't applicable to me because I no longer smoked pot or did drugs.

The rules sounded random, but the explanations were reason-able. When some of us questioned Simon, he suggested we not take the rules on faith but verify whether they helped us and "our inner development." Fair enough. He also emphasized that membership in School was voluntary and that we weren't obligated to stay. (It didn't occur to me that it was anything but voluntary until he made this peculiar remark.)

Orientation was over and we went into the main room where class had already begun. At the head of the room were the teachers, Fred and Priscilla. They were in their late thirties to early forties.

Fred Mindel had thick white hair and wore gold-rimmed glasses. He had a large frame and a booming, nasal voice that made him sound like an opera singer with a cold. His appearance reminded me of Tom Snyder, the talk show host from the 1970s and 1980s. A former civil rights attorney in California, he changed professions and became a chiropractor and kinesiologist. He had a nervous tic that caused him to blink and stammer. To add to the odd spectacle was the sight of Hazel scuttling about the room, tripping over herself to refill their coffee mugs, restock their plates of finger foods, and clear away abandoned crumpled napkins. I couldn't follow the discussion, and no effort was made to integrate the newcomers into the conversation (indeed nobody acknowledged us when we entered the room). We were basically lost as they discussed Peter Ouspensky's *The Psychology of Man's Possible Evolution*, a series of lectures fundamental to George Gurdjieff's system.

After about an hour, I'd had enough of Fred and my uncomfortable squeaky chair. I couldn't follow the inscrutable discussion and there was nothing remotely interesting about this. I couldn't understand what in the world Heather and Bruce thought was so sublime and magical about these teachers. But just as I stood to leave, Fred fell silent, stopping the class. "Oh, Spencer, you have to leave early?" Embarrassed that he'd noticed me and knew my name, I replied, "Yes, I have somewhere to go." He asked my "impressions" of the class. I politely lied that it was "deep." He nodded and then asked, "So you like the Stones?" He was reacting to the fact that I was carrying my bass guitar gig bag because I had a rehearsal later that night. I told him I did. He appeared to have no further questions. I turned and left, not inclined to return.

Second Class

How does one's memory hold up when recalling the tiny decisions, the simple actions, the daily motivations behind consequential events that happened long ago—or even recently? Why did I merge into the left lane (when I could have stayed where I was) and smack another car? Why did I return for a second night of classes after the disappointing first night? I've long believed that I need to have a reasonable, rational answer for why I returned for the second night. I'm not alone here—many of us engage in this Monday-morning quarterbacking, this second-guessing. Any good trial lawyer will tell you that in recalling events, people just make things up because memories are faulty, and we like to sound reasonable and rational even though we aren't. And so, we end up with revisions or gaps (or just make stuff up). Some of us are lazy and reference things like "fate" or we claim that the "universe conspired" against us or for us. The question of "what made me go into that bar where I ended up meeting my future wife" could be as simple and unromantic as needing to pee and hence ignoring the "Restroom for Patrons Only" sign.

Why did I go back the second night? There was the connection and the knowing looks between Heather and Bruce. There was the philosophy they were studying: I had missed the intellectual rigors of my liberal arts education. There was the possibility that if I didn't go back Bruce might hound me again. There was Hazel's soul mate remark. There was my boredom with my life: it was the same old thing. Also, I liked the idea of an exclusive secret, and the experiment was only for a month. What did I have to lose? And, there was a phone call to my office the morning after class from a stranger named Morton.

Morton introduced himself as a "friend" from School and said he would be my "sustainer." He explained that a sustainer is an older student who I'd be able to talk with outside class, one on one, about anything discussed in class, the readings we would be doing, and anything else. His voice was kind. He was formal and polite ("*Good morning, Spencer,*" "*How are you, Spencer?*")—like Heather and Hazel.

He asked, "So Spencer, how was your first night of class last night?"

"It was OK," I said.

"Oh, I'm glad to hear that. I hope it fed you."

He asked if I had any questions about what was said. I told him that it was all new and I'd had trouble following it. Morton said that students would be asked to purchase certain study books that would help make things clearer, but that it was understandable that it had been hard to follow.

"It was just your first night, Spencer, that's totally normal," he tried to reassure me. Morton detected my reticence and changed the subject. He asked me about my personal life: occupation, where I was from, lived. I gave him my background and I asked him the same. He told me he had gone to Yale and was working at an advertising agency.

His good nature put me at ease. I was again struck how polite every one of them seemed. Plus, he was astute and quick-witted. So, I opened up to him a little. By the end of the call, I determined that I couldn't judge School by one night. Morton suggested that I come for a few weeks. It never felt like he was trying to push me or overtly convince me to come back. He was just nice to me, like all of them.

I came straight down from the office, taking the 6 train to Canal and Lafayette. I arrived in Chinatown, where it smelled like egg rolls and rotting fish and my shirt was drenched with sweat. I walked west on the south side of Canal Street, passing the motionless men and women sitting in stalls offering Louis Vuitton bags and Rolex watches. I turned left on a deserted Broadway, moon gates down for the night. I found my way to the Space. *What am I doing here?* The air-conditioning wasn't working, and the windows were open with overhead fans blowing around the hot air. Fred wasn't teaching, Simon was, along with Priscilla. I liked Simon. He wasn't as strange as Fred. We spent the evening speaking about the "Three Centers." According to Gurdjieff, we had an intellectual center, an emotional center, and a moving center. They each corresponded to thoughts, feelings, and sensations that could often be in line with each other or opposed. For instance, Simon said, we might be feeling sad at a funeral but be thinking about what we are going to be having for lunch. I could relate to this because I'm always thinking about my next meal, even during meals. To test the theory—*Oh, I liked this idea of verifying things*—Simon had some exercises he wanted us to practice. He suggested something called the "self-observation" exercise. Through self-observation of these centers, it was claimed, one could become not merely aware of one's "machine" but eventually become fully conscious. Simon wanted us to buy a small notebook and record observations at 10:00 a.m., 2:00 p.m., and 6:00 p.m. of whatever we were thinking, feeling, and sensing in those respective centers. Simon also asked us to purchase two books by Ouspensky, *The Psychology of Man's Possible Evolution* and *In Search of the Miraculous,* and to put on plain book covers to ensure invisibility.

Barnes & Noble didn't sell these books. I had to go to a shop in the Village called East West Books that played new age music, smelled of sandalwood incense, and sold crystals, Buddhas, yoga mats, wheat germ, and books with titles like *The Dancing Wu Li Masters* and *The Secret Language of Birthdays.* That weekend I went to Long Island, and I settled into a beach chair with my fresh, covered copy of Ouspensky's *In Search of the Miraculous.* Ouspensky was a student of Gurdjieff, and this book recounted studying under his teacher. I wasn't impressed with what Ouspensky had to say. I shouldn't have been surprised that a book thus titled would leave me searching for something, anything. Ouspensky specialized in outlandish statements, dressing up bluster and bravado as evidence. For instance, he asserted that the universe was based upon "vibrations" which emanated from an "Absolute" through the galaxies to our solar system to earth and all the way down to man. It is one thing to speak this way allegorically. For Ouspensky, however, these assertions were "scientific truths" which he insisted could be "verified" by an individual person because "man is really a microcosmos of the universe." His book, written in 1949, makes no mention or acknowledgment of things such as Newton's laws of motion and universal gravitation nor Einstein's Theory of Relativity. Worse, Ouspensky was apparently stuck in a pre-Galileo geocentric model of the universe with the earth as the center; Ouspensky apparently had no problem with Galileo's head rolling off the chopping block. My mind drifted off to the endless ocean, the surface of which—like a blanket—obscured the world below.

Ouspensky, however, seemed to confirm Bruce's claim that Gurdjieff's system revolved around "schools of esoteric knowledge," which he asserted existed since the "dawn of time." This was a good thing. He argued that man is "asleep" and could only "awaken" through esoteric schools with "real teachers" (such as himself) through the system of the Work which he claimed was a combination of Eastern and Western spiritual "ways." He called his system the "Fourth Way," which he claimed was unlike the three ways of the ascetics (fakirs, yogis, monks) in that the Fourth Way adherents did not need to leave society in order to attain consciousness. Gurdjieff established schools in Europe and the United States and had many followers, including some renowned people such as Frank Lloyd Wright. He also influenced several who became teachers and writers of his Work. This was a world I hadn't known about.

Aside from his fascination with his own brand of cosmology, Ouspensky asserted in *The Psychology of Man's Possible Evolution* that, contrary to popular belief, psychology was not an invention of modernity, but had existed since ancient times in various traditions. He argued that ancient psychology was far more advanced than modern psychology because it didn't just analyze man but proffered that man had the possibility to evolve into a more advanced and perfect being.

Freud's notions of ego, id, and superego had no place in Ouspensky's cosmology, nor did the unconscious or subconscious.[2] Rather, as noted, man was said to have three centers from which all thoughts, feelings, and movements emanated. In addition, man was a multiplicity with different groups of "I's." The goal of the Work was to help us to create a single I or to become a unity and rise above all the contradictions and inconsistencies that plague man and mankind and which lead to misunderstanding, war, and suffering. The Work taught, however, that not everyone could—or would even want to—obtain perfection—i.e., to become what is known as "Man Number 7." But if enough people could reach this height, then they could save civilization. (In this regard, later on, Fred liked to remind us that because the Work was not for everyone, we should be careful to guard against feeling superior to people outside the Work. "You are different, but you are not better," Fred warned us.)

During another call with Morton (he called me every day to check in on me), I expressed some of my reservations about the books. He listened and didn't argue or talk me into anything. He agreed that the ideas were "different from any other way of thinking."

So, I kept going. I told myself it was an experiment. Something I was doing just to do it. For fun. For the story. Like taking French lessons or learning tap dancing. And even though only about six of us from the first night were still coming to class, I wanted to complete the month's experiment because I had made that commitment to Bruce, whom I would still see at the North River. Plus, what Hazel said, and those glances—the friendship between Bruce and Heather. But a few weeks into my experiment I confronted a crisis, and that's when things changed.

---

2   This view that modern psychology was basically a bleak, one-dimensional study permeated a lot of School, and it was often discussed in derogatory terms. We were encouraged to discard popular opinions about modern psychology and focus instead on ancient psychology espoused by the Work. We were told not to see therapists, a rule I eventually broke, with significant consequences.

It happened one late afternoon. My boss, Rockhead, poked his head into my office, "Spencer, meet me in Cogswell's office in fifteen minutes." My guts churned. The previous week my assistant accidentally faxed legal papers to the other side, spoiling a surprise lawsuit. It wasn't a big deal and not my fault, but judging from Rockhead's explosive reaction when he heard about it, I was half expecting to be fired for it. I was half right. Cogswell, the managing partner, spoke from behind his empty mahogany desk. "Your work has been disappointing. The firm is letting you go."

The wind was knocked out of me, yet I was able to eke out, "Because of the fax?"

"Not entirely, but it didn't help," chimed Rockhead.

I reasoned, "But I've done good work. I've only had good reports from everyone."

No response from these two. With no explanation, I was given three months until my last day.[3]

I was like a zombie. I left Cogswell's office; I took the elevator downstairs; I walked home that early evening down Park Avenue; I passed people in business clothes hurrying someplace; the sticky July air; acrid fumes from trucks lined up for the Queens–Midtown Tunnel; the whirling thoughts; dread. But when I passed the building where my dad worked in the 1960s (on Park Avenue South and Twenty-seventh Street), something hit me. I can start my own law office. I'm going to hang out my own shingle. Why should I waste my time working for anyone else? Joel had his own practice and an extra office in his suite. I felt hopeful.

When I got up to my apartment, I didn't want to call any of my friends or my family with this news. It was embarrassing. Too much to explain. Thoughts too jumbled. I headed to class. It was hard to concentrate during the first half of class, and I don't remember what was discussed. But about halfway through class, Fred said in a welcoming way, "So, now it's time for any questions about how to apply

---

3   I did not know—and my bosses did not tell me—that the firm (which had been founded more than a hundred years ago) was in the process of dissolving. It closed its doors for good the day I left.

the Work principles to your life. This is called 'Being Work'—where you can grow your being from the Work." I had an explosive need to get this off my chest.

I stood and said, "Fred, today I was let go from my job. It was an unexpected shock." As I spoke, I could sense the sixty other students' empathy and concern. Fred and Priscilla were intently taking me in as though this was of the utmost importance to them, the way Bruce and Heather had listened to me. The coffee urns were bubbling in the back. All eyes were on me. Cigarette smoke filled the room, ashtrays on people's laps, the fragrant lilies set beside Priscilla and Fred. But it was still, quiet, inviting. I opened up. I spoke about my anger, fear, doubts. Priscilla became misty eyed. I continued, "I'm going to open my own law office within the next three months." Smiles lit up the room. Fred interrupted me with applause and the room joined. My heart surged. The affection from this group of strangers, like a salve, made me love them. A wave of loving-kindness: how can I not love these people back in my time of need?

The applause ended and Fred looked directly at me, the room now silent. He slowly intoned, "There is a Jewish proverb that 'every apparent curse is a hidden blessing.' Losing your job looks like a curse if you approach the event from 'life thinking.' But if you look at this event from the perspective of the Work, you will see that it is a blessing. With the Work, we can transform the negative into the positive. Opening your office is a great Aim. Anything is possible. With the force of the Work, you will have the wind in your sails." He stopped and he gave me a broad smile. Despite Fred's quirky tics, he had a powerful presence. There was an unmistakable aura about him. He seemed to come from a different realm. His command of Work ideas and the reverential treatment accorded him by the other students reinforced his appeal, brilliance, and mystery. Fred's acknowledgment of me, and his advice to me in this public setting, was like the rabbi's benediction at the end of the service, with arms outstretched as the congregation bows their heads. I was being protected, blessed by the Work. Fred suddenly reminded me of driving with my father—strong, wise, protective, and comforting.

The flow continued: One at a time, several classmates stood up and testified about how the Work and Aims had not only helped them with crises but also with achieving success and finding meaning. One by one they stood up and comforted me with "Second Line of Work"—helping your neighbor. Ned, an NYU graduate and painter who sold high-end carpets, said that "this could be the best thing that ever happened to you." Gloria, whose family owned the largest beer brewery in the world, said that the Work was a "blessing." Barry managed one of the biggest construction companies in the city and told me that with the Work I would become "rich beyond my dreams." Bonnie was getting her MBA from Columbia in marketing and announced that the "force of the Work" would sustain me. Thomas, the heir to one of the biggest cosmetic companies, shouted out, "Congratulations," and led a standing ovation like I had just won a gold medal at the Olympics.

There were others who offered support: Raymond (an actuary from Pittsburgh), Sam (a writer with a Southern accent), Emma (a yoga instructor from Colorado), Marion (an accountant from Maine who favored Gucci bags), Harold (physician, teacher, and author). These were people I barely knew and with whom I'd never had direct conversations, let alone their phone numbers—I'd only seen them in class, where the rules forbade us from speaking before or after the teachers were leading class. After the testimonials, Fred said, "Spencer, these are your 'Essence Friends'—we are all here to help with your Aim." By now, I had completely forgotten that I had been canned hours earlier. I felt the love. I felt the power and the force of this small group. It was an extraordinary experience unmatched by anything I could have imagined. It was irresistible. Nobody that I knew—or had access to—could have cheered me up like this and inspired me.

When Fred and the others mentioned that thing about "a great Aim," they had something specific in mind. Fred had recently explained it. The other cosmological ideas of the Work—the "Absolute," vibrations shooting down the universe, and the "Table of Hydrogens"—were about as interesting as the comings and goings of Bigfoot. But I loved the idea of "Aim," also known as the "Law of the Octave." It was called the Law of the Octave because it's based on the eight-note musical scale. The idea posits that any enterprise (like writing an essay, or baking a cake, or learning German) involves an eight-note process with two specific points where the enterprise can collapse unless the actor does what the Work teaches: specifically, something called "Self-Remembering." Self-Remembering was the most important idea of the Work, its foundational idea—like what a Big Mac is to McDonald's. As Fred spoke, I realized that he was exceptionally brilliant. He had a first-rate mind and was a great orator. He explained, "Try to think of all the Aims you've had in your life. And then try to recall where the project or dream or endeavor veered off the path. Think of the person who sets out to be an artist but ends up in disappointment and disillusionment getting a job as an accountant and giving up his art. With Aim and Self-Remembering—which are only possible in the Work with the aid of School—only then can someone (barring luck) achieve his goal with consciousness." This example registered with me, and my recent frustration as having ended up as Bartleby the Scrivener and not as Atticus Finch.

Fred continued, "Self-Remembering is when you *remember yourself*," emphasizing the last two words in his baritone and placing both hands on the center of his chest. "Most of us don't remember ourselves and are not conscious." This was it. Questions for clarification were met with polite but firm retorts and witticisms counseling inquisitors to try to do it, and that it just can't be intellectually explained but must be practiced for a long time in order to become effective, and that eventually it would lead to full consciousness of everything. The more Fred threw this back at the class to figure it out, the more he persuaded me (and other classmates, who nodded in agreement). This was a challenge, a puzzle, and a key to something potentially valuable. Not earth shattering, but certainly of value. Self-Remembering sounded like praying but without reference to a deity. I could remember when I was younger and had a more optimistic, and innocent view of life. Perhaps Self-Remembering was as simple as remembering those feelings. Either way, Fred was not going to lay it out any clearer.[4]

---

4   If Fred's definition of Self-Remembering was vague, he had good reason. According to Gurdjieff's apostle Ouspensky, even the great man himself

I decided I would continue past my one-month experiment: there would now be a monthly tuition of $300, which was paid quarterly, in advance. In cash please, fifties only. No problem. It is well worth it. After all, I was starting to believe that the force of the Work and Aim might help my career. At the end of this evening, I stood up in class and thanked Fred and Priscilla and my classmates for their support. Fred smiled and said, "The Work works."

---

discussed it in the most inscrutable terms: "In order really to observe oneself one must first of all *remember oneself,*" Ouspensky quotes Gurdjieff as having said. "Try to *remember yourselves* when you observe yourselves and later on tell me the results. Only those results will have any value that are accompanied by self-remembering. Otherwise you yourselves do not exist in your observations. In which case what are all your observations worth?"

The Work Works

I was reinvigorated, filled with a new sense of purpose. I was high for months. It was a good thing because I needed to rent an office, needed a phone line, needed to learn how to type on my new IBM DOS personal computer. I needed to get clients. So, I networked over lunches and dinners, I renewed old connections, and I generated my first client, then a second, then a third, all before I even opened my office. I was blessed. I had the force of the Work.

I gave weekly progress reports to the whole class. Every time I was given more help, encouragement, affirmations. I walked out of classes feeling invincible. The Work, Aim, and my sense of connection with members of School were becoming essential to my life. Fred said I owed what was happening in my life to the Work, that I was "indebted" to the Work. He was right, I felt it. He also said I needed to develop an "internal gratitude" to the Work and my teachers and that it was imperative to express it in class. He explained, "otherwise your connection to School is weakened and the Work will *not* work." I didn't doubt him. The mystery, the wonder, the invisible force, an unexplained power that could be traced through esoteric schools made sense to me now. This sentiment was reinforced by the experience of a class full of people who had this shared belief, and it became intoxicating. Heather's words, her emotions, her beauty, the way she had looked at Bruce, what they said about teachers, it came back to me, "To change yourself is like nothing else. To find the truth and freedom is sublime." Morton echoed this: "Spencer, gratitude in the Work means something different than in life. It's not just about saying or feeling it—it's about doing it—doing your exercises, following the rules, doing the readings, coming to class, speaking in class, and being sincere with the teachers." And then he said to me, in a serious tone, "Once you lose your connection with School, the force of the Work is lost." I didn't take this as a threat; I took this to heart.

To be sure, there were other things happening outside School that I attributed to the powers of the Work and strengthened my devotion. I started dating someone seriously for the first time in years. I had known and liked Kathy since high school, but now—suddenly—she was showing interest in me, and we were having a great romance. Similarly, on my thirtieth birthday, my old friends threw me a surprise party, something that had never happened before. I was making new friends who were also working musicians who I admired, and they were inviting me to gig with them. Law clients were rolling in. Life was good. The Work was working.

There was something else that kept me coming back to classes: I enjoyed talking about the ideas of Gurdjieff and Ouspensky. The discussions were stimulating, the students and teachers were inquisitive, and I got to study and read something besides the law. It was like all my favorite college classes, except practical.

And through it all, I told no one about School. Like *Fight Club*: "The first rule about fight club is you don't talk about fight club. The second rule about fight club is you don't talk about fight club." It was easy. I didn't want to talk with anyone outside School about it, anyone who would question the classes or my involvement. It was not only thrilling to have a secret life, like Clark Kent, but I began to believe that it had to be kept a secret for its powers to work for me. And I similarly understood that the secrets teachers and sustainers kept from me (i.e., the history and background of School) had to be maintained for its powers to work over me. We were all careful not to ask questions. But it made me more curious, always hoping to discover more information. All this intrigue was alluring, exciting, like a book you couldn't put down.

Fred started class one night saying, "Let's begin with any and all questions about the Work." I jumped to my feet and spoke: "Fred, when I first came a few months ago I was distrustful of School. Now I'm really getting and embracing the Work. It's happened so fast and it's hard to reconcile. It's almost as if I'm being brainwashed." Fred cut me off, enraged, shouting "*Slander!!!*" His face turned crimson, eyes blinked wildly, body shook like he was having a seizure.

The air went out of the room, out of my lungs. I felt light-headed, my heart beat hard in that moment. Priscilla gently broke the ice while Fred silently boiled. "It's a good point, Spencer, but reserve your judgment while you verify your experience."

Morton called me the next morning. He asked me about class. I told him about my gaffe and Fred's reaction. Morton seemed to take it in stride. "It's good to let those voices speak," he said. "But do you really think that you—a bright person, a lawyer—could be brainwashed?" I agreed he had a good point. Morton said, "Falling for the Work is a little like falling in love—it's mysterious." This sounded like an apt analogy. But I had never seen Fred—let alone any teacher—lose his cool before or attack any other student. It was verbal punishment. He humiliated me. Why, I asked, would Fred do that? Morton listened, sympathetic. He didn't try to push or convince me. He just stated his feelings: "We are learning to evolve. Struggle is part of change. Like working out at the gym. Classes are a place to struggle. It's called 'struggle without destruction,' and it's really a beautiful thing. Teachers are our guides. They may sometimes say things that ruffle your 'false personality,' but they will never hurt the *real you*." Then he joked, "Spencer, I can assure you that you are not being brainwashed. Take it from me: I was already brainwashed by Yale University, and I wouldn't let it happen again. But seriously, use your own judgment and verify for yourself whether you're being brainwashed. Don't take anyone's word for it." I took this as a kind of an acknowledgment that Fred went too far and an assurance that nobody was trying to trick me. My involvement was of my own free will.

Fred started the next class by reading from *In Search of the Miraculous:* "'Man has no individual I. But there are, instead, hundreds and thousands of separate small I's, often entirely unknown to one another, never coming into contact, or, on the contrary, hostile to each other, mutually exclusive and incompatible. Each minute, each moment, man is saying or thinking 'I.' And each time his I is different. Just now it was a thought, now it is a desire, now a sensation, now another thought, and so on, endlessly. Man is a plurality. Man's name is legion.'" Fred continued reading, "'We are thoroughly prisoners of this unruly crowd of I's. It's like a person with multiple personalities.'" Then he put down the book, squinted, and said to me directly, "It's critical that you let all of your I's speak when you're in class so that they can be given voice and seen for what they are." And then he added this, which seemed to be the entire point, "Certain I's in you are slanderous, or hateful, or even murderous. But you—as a person—your Essence—you are none of those things. This is an important distinction." I got it; Fred was talking to my slanderous I's. I understood.

Morton called me the next morning. "Spencer, you have a great mind and are doing so well in School. Keep up the good work." I let it go. How could I not? It really was like falling in love.

Class Outside of Class

The following week there was a luxury charter bus idling in front of the Space and Fred and Simon ushering us into it. When we settled in, Fred stood in the front of the bus and said, "We are going to have a special class tonight—it's a class outside of class. Remember, everything in School is for learning."

We drove about an hour to northern Westchester County until we arrived at what appeared to be an old lodge hall, hidden down a long unpaved driveway, deep in the woods. It was dark and the leaves were already gone, giving the property a spooky feeling with moonlight streaming between the naked branches. The air was chillier there. We pulled up to the front door. Fred said, "You have all earned this class, and it will help us 'cross an interval.'"

We exited the bus in a single file and walked straight into the lodge. A live band struck up, playing loud and fast country western music. We received a hero's welcome from our sustainers (about twenty-five of them were there) who grabbed us to join them in a square dance. The entire lodge was decorated in a western theme. The sustainers were decked out in cowboy boots, cowboy hats, and bandannas. Extra bandannas were handed out to us. We square danced and afterward we mingled and had drinks. After months of being in the formal settings of a class, it was strange, wonderful to be socializing with each other, especially in such a festive way.

We sat down for a feast of home-cooked BBQ, all prepared by our sustainers.[5] This was a celebration of School, the Work, and mostly the deep friendships we were developing. Incredibly, it was a party that I couldn't talk about with anyone not there. During dinner, Fred stood to speak. He said that it was a glorious evening, and he wanted us to "remember" the evening and feel "gratitude for what brings us together."

After about six hours of partying, well past midnight, we were back on the bus, this time with many of our sustainers, and returned to the city. I woke up the next morning satisfied, light, happy, and easy; it was one the best nights I'd ever had with some of the most amazing people around.

But I sensed the pattern. One class could be inspiring, mesmerizing, glorious, and then the next one could be harsh, tumultuous, chaotic. The teachers could be warm, funny, and loving or testy and truculent. There was no telling what kind of class we were walking into, so we got used to walking on eggshells. The switch could happen within one class, on a dime. This was keeping us on our toes. Morton had explained it earlier—the Work and classes involve struggle. I came to see it this way. We all did. Struggle was a necessary part of this process of evolution and awakening. Additionally, harsh things could be said to someone, but it was almost always followed up by softer treatment, even praise or love—a spoonful of sugar to help the medicine go down. And if you couldn't take this way of learning, then School was not for you.

---

5   A note about sustainers: they were students who had been in School longer (i.e., "older students"). Their class met on Tuesday and Thursday nights, and my class met on Monday and Wednesdays, although later we switched nights with them. Their class also had about sixty students, though not everyone in that class was a sustainer. The classes never mingled, and there were many students in School whom I never met. Teachers never discussed or even acknowledged the existence of the other classes even though it became clear after a couple of years that they existed. Including the Boston branch—which I learned of later in my tenure and which had about one hundred students— there were approximately 250 students in School at any given time. Over the decades, there were probably a few thousand people who attended classes.

Struggle was part of it, and I accepted it, even began to embrace it. I was free to leave at any time. Nobody pressured me to stay in School. I wanted to be there.

That year's Christmas Class was planned as a party in the Space, and we were to decorate it and prepare some hors d'oeuvres and drinks for the teachers and just our class. I volunteered to be the DJ. We met after class ended. Hazel asked me to show her the song list. When she saw "Over the Rainbow," she turned to me and said accusingly, "That song shouldn't have been included, Spencer. Fred told you it was a silly, sentimental song." Up to now, Hazel had only spoken to me with respect and kindness. But she was making this up and I had no idea why. Fred never said a word to me about any songs. Her face twisted up as I explained her mistake. She lost it. She shrieked, stopping the sixty people in the room, "You're lying, Spencer." I stood there dumbfounded, speechless. I was pissed, but I'd seen this movie and knew how it ended. I wasn't gonna win this. My thoughts raced back and forth. I racked my brain to try to remember when Fred said this—he hadn't. But I wanted Hazel's fit to stop more than I wanted to be right. But again, maybe she was right—her vehemence only seemed to buttress that possibility in my mind. And then there was her position of authority and her ability to "see me." I couldn't afford to anger her anymore, afraid of unknown repercussions. Then again, maybe I was lying to Hazel. I couldn't think straight. Sixty people were silently watching.

So, I said it: "You're right, Hazel. I remember now. I must have been asleep." She relented. It was over. Hazel turned and hugged me. She congratulated me for "the breakthrough" to see what a liar "Spencer Schneider" is. (We referred to our given name to distinguish between our false self and our nameless real self.) So, it had become fact: I had lied. I thanked her again. But at the same time, a part of me was seething that I had made this false confession. The conflict was heightened by the fact that my classmates admired "my brave work" and they showered me with praise.

A few months later, in the spring of 1990, we were greeted on the street in front of the Space by a dozen sustainers. They walked us to the subway station on Canal and Broadway. We boarded a train, got out at the Sheepshead Bay stop, walked to the docks, boarded a chartered fishing boat, and spent the night fishing about ten miles out in the Atlantic Ocean. When the sun started to rise over the Atlantic Ocean, with the lit-up New York skyline in the north, we went up to the deck where speakers were set up blasting the Blue Danube waltz by Strauss. We took partners and waltzed for an hour until we docked. The gulls flying above, the smell of the water, the swaying of the boat, the waltzing, the best friends you could ever have, melding into one giant lovefest. This was another memorable and lovely evening, buried in the early years of my involvement with School.

The Rules of Evolution

One night, I came late to class. I'd been waiting for NYNEX to repair my office phone. I arrived, sweating, and stressed out, at 7:20 p.m. Toward the end of class, Fred turned to me and said, "Spencer, I noticed you were late to class. Why?" The blood rushed to my face and all eyes were on me. I stammered through a clumsy response, trying to explain. Fred shook his head, "No, that is life thinking. You were late because your valuation of School is still low, and you have a weak being." I became queasy and light-headed. The room started to look hazy except for Fred, who was focused intently on me. He was looking right into me and could read my thoughts. I was naked, vulnerable, but safe. What he was saying was probably true, much like when Hazel called me out. He continued, "If your valuation—your love of the Work—were what it should be, you would have been here on time. If you had a strong being, you would have found a way to make sure you were here on time and that your phone was installed at the same time."

I sat there in silence, trying to let this penetrate. On one hand, I thought Fred was being a dick. But having just been down this road, I decided to give in. Maybe he was right. Maybe my "objection" to his remarks only proved that he was right. Maybe I could have insisted that NYNEX show up another night or somehow in my subconscious I had scheduled it on a class night because I didn't value class enough. Or maybe I should have had someone else be there for the NYNEX man so I could get to class. If I had a stronger being, I could have afforded a nighttime secretary to do this. The list went on. I thanked Fred.

When class was over, I did something that students were not allowed to do after class (and that litigants don't do with judges): I approached Fred. Up close he was tall and hulking, an intimidating presence. I saw that he had a scar running down his nose. "Fred, you were right about what you said to me, how did you know that?" Without missing a beat, and without castigating me for approaching him, he said, "Because I *know* beings." He patted me on the shoulder and walked away. I stood in awe that he had imparted his wisdom to me. Other students came by and patted me on the shoulder as well. Sam gave me a bear hug, and said, "Spencer, I've never seen the receptive and willing side of you. It makes me happy. It's so different from the angry and cynical 'Spencer Schneider' from when you first came. I'm proud of you, man." I felt the magic, the power, that Fred and this Work possessed.

A student named Robbie had missed a week of classes because he had the flu. Robbie was an accountant, had combed-back slick hair, kept to himself, and wore heavy gold jewelry. He was a nice man. But when he came back to class, Fred questioned his absence, telling him he missed out on a "peak time to work on himself." Robbie and everyone did a double take. Fred said that according to the Work everyone is in "False Personality" all the time as opposed to "True Personality" or "Essence." But when you are ill, or tired for lack of sleep, you don't have the energy to put up pretenses which keep you from "hearing the Work." Therefore, according to the Work, when you are ill or tired, you "hear the Work better." Fred said that nobody could ever miss class unless they were seriously ill. Robbie listened passively as Fred spoke. We never saw Robbie again after that night.

We were all so afraid that we would be publicly chastised if we missed even a single class that we showed up no matter how sick we were, the unfortunate result being that we constantly caught the flu and colds from each other. One time I came to class despite severe abdominal pain. When was class was over, I went to the emergency room, where I had immediate surgery to remove my gallbladder.

One night, a student named Jeb got up during class to head for the bathroom. Fred interrupted class and said to him, "Are you sure you want to miss what is about to be said?" Poor Jeb was embarrassed, and I was afraid he would wet himself. Fred said, "nothing is ever repeated in class and once it's missed it's gone forever; it's a 'law' that people miss the most important thing they need to hear when they were not present in class." This was in reference to an anecdote in *In Search of the Miraculous* in which Ouspensky said he would have walked miles through a storm to get to a class taught by Gurdjieff rather than possibly miss some life-changing piece of wisdom. Fred suggested that when people had the urge to go to the bathroom that they "remember themselves" and not jump up but try to listen to what is being said at that moment because it was exactly the help they needed to hear which would change their life. This kind of put the kibosh on peeing during class. Who would go? If you did, Fred would almost always mention your name while you were peeing saying "I wish [fill in the name of the urinator] had heard this." And the class would laugh uproariously, which the urinator undoubtedly heard in the bathroom. "That's Fred Law," said someone. More laughing. When the urinator came back to his or her seat Fred stopped the class and said, "I wished you had heard what we said about [fill in the supposedly great thing the urinator missed]. Mechanicality makes us miss our life." Everyone would snicker and hold it in.

The rule of invisibility extended to everyone, especially spouses of students. Fred instructed married students to say nothing about their nights out to their spouses except that it was "private" and to please respect that. If the spouse persisted, they were to say, "it's none of your business." Fred said that marriage didn't mean you couldn't have your own space, your own private, separate life. He insisted that it was vital for people's "evolution" to handle it this way. Firmly. Very. Everyone complied with it. Women generally had more success with this than men, but not much. In two instances at least, male students had their newlywed spouses leave them for saying it was none of their business. Fred either blamed these students for failing to "be in the right place internally" or blamed the spouse for being "against" the student.

We were surprised when Dolores, a well-liked and active participant in class, hadn't been to class for a few weeks. No announcement was made of her whereabouts. It was like she had fallen off the earth. Concerned, another student named Mark asked Fred during class why she hadn't been coming to class. Fred's face scrunched up like he'd eaten a sour pickle. He took a sip of coffee and gathered himself. He asked Mark, "How will it help you in your evolution to know the answer to this question?" Mark mumbled something, nodded to Fred, and sat himself down. Fred explained that Dolores had been asked to leave School, that she had a "low valuation" of the Work, and had violated the rule of invisibility. He said that he "wished her well" but that we were not to contact Dolores. If she were to contact any of us, he said, we were not to engage and should let Fred know if she had. After this exchange—and Fred's response to Mark—nobody ever asked about a student who had left.

Fred gave us two new exercises to do every day: "Self-Sensing" and the "Recollection Exercise." When the morning alarm went off, we were to remain in bed and Self-Sense, which meant to remain still and sense the air in the room, the covers on your body, your breathing, your heartbeat, the light in the room and so on. In addition, before we went to sleep at night, we were to recollect every event of the day, one by one, starting from the moment we awoke until bedtime: this was the Recollection Exercise. By this, our days began and ended with the Work. Without fail, I fell back asleep within half a minute of Self-Sensing as did every other student. We were exhausted. The Recollection Exercise kept us up. Fred explained that we needed to redouble our efforts. "Grow your being," he would say.

Let's Meet Sharon and Robert

Remember those times in grade school when some stranger—usually a man in a tie—suddenly appears, takes a seat in the back of the class, and just sits there? Silent, observing. The teacher doesn't introduce them. A distracting presence, a mystery, an elephant in the room. Rumors fly: it's a spy, a cop, worries, anxiety, put on best behavior. So, when a stranger suddenly arrived to observe our class in the summer of 1990—twelve months after my first class—I was conveyed back to grade school.

Her outlandish appearance made it creepier and more troubling—a little scary. She had thick bright orange hair tied in a bun on top of her head and wore heavy gold jewelry and a formal floor-length dress. She had pale white skin, deep-set cerulean eyes, and a nose akin to a raptor's beak. She stood no more than five feet, two inches, and was heavyset. Fred led her out of the teachers' office from the back of the classroom as we sat in our seats waiting for class to begin. She took an empty seat in the back row. We pretended not to notice her, but we didn't stop stealing glances. I thought she looked positively nuts. She said nothing. She scanned the room, inspecting us, inspecting our teachers. Her mere presence violated the safety of our School. There was something imperial, authoritative about her. Yet, Fred and Priscilla opened class as if nothing were different. The more I tried not to think about her, the more I did. The more everyone tried to act like nothing was different, the more different it was. She listened intently, expressionless. She was clearly too old to be a potential student, a good fifteen years older than Fred, Priscilla, Simon, and our other teacher, Robert. This was a mystery. Was she sent from headquarters? Make her go away.

Robert had started to teach class shortly after I began. He and Fred alternated nights, but in no apparent pattern. We were never told in advance who was teaching. We were always kept in suspense.

Robert was in his mid-forties. He stood about five feet, seven inches, and had thick dark straight hair that he wore short and parted. He had a heavy black beard. He was a wealthy entrepreneur. He smoked a musky tobacco in a pipe with which he was constantly fiddling. He wore chinos and Brooks Brother oxford shirts and a jacket with elbow pads. He also wore suspenders, which I had noticed Morton also wore, as did some of the other sustainers. Robert reminded me of my college intellectual history professor. And he spoke with supreme confidence. He was quick to smile and had a deep voice but with a faint occasional lisp that almost sounded like a whistle. His eyes were dark and his manner was relaxed, unlike Fred. But, like Fred, he was brilliant and a natural orator. And like Fred, he had a way of letting you know that he was smarter than you, but you didn't mind it.

My first interaction with Robert came when I was seated in the back of the class wearing a baseball cap. Robert was leading the class with a relatively new teacher, Maude Frankel, who chain-smoked and wore a permanent scowl. Maude had been married to Simon. Seeing me in the back row alone, Maude interrupted the class and said, "Spencer, why are you sitting back there wearing a hat? Come on up front." I explained that I was under the weather and didn't want to get anyone else sick. Sensing my unease and perhaps to take the lead, Robert came to my aid, remarking to Maude, "I sometimes wear a baseball cap when I'm sick." He continued in his deep voice, in comforting tones, "Spencer, I know you are not feeling well. But here is a great opportunity to go against your mechanical False Personality and perhaps create a new avenue in yourself." He had my attention, and continued, "So in the spirit of doing something good for yourself, why don't you take a seat closer to the rest of the class. Nobody will be afraid to catch your cold." People chuckled. "And take off your hat too. Then see how you feel and speak about it to us. This will be a great way to verify the Work." I complied, grateful to Robert for defending me and helping me to shed my old ways.

Two weeks after the orange-haired stranger appeared in the back of the room, she returned. But this time, her arm draped in Fred's arm, she walked up to the front of the class and sat in a leather recliner between Fred and Priscilla. She wore the same style of long flowing dress and jewelry, but this time she sported black Converse sneakers. I was not quite as uneasy about her now because of the deference that Fred and Priscilla showed her—clearly, she was important. But I was baffled by how weird she was—preposterously dressed and man-nered. She looked out at the room and smiled at us. She said hello and introduced herself as Sharon. Then, she said, in a falsetto singsongy voice, "The Work teaches that if you use your sexual energy for self-glory, you will drain yourself and become tired and eventually lose the Work. You cannot work on yourself without sexual energy. Sex is sacred and will raise your level of being. Do not leak your sex energy. Do not masturbate. Use your sex energy for conception and creating a soul. Make love to your lover and not to yourself. Ultimately you want to make love to the Work and make her your lover."

I didn't need to look around the room to see the discomfort. I sat between Emma and Raymond, neither of whom were breathing any-more. Some of us lit up cigarettes. Fred and Priscilla were, however, in deep contemplation, taking this in as though it were the words of Christ himself. Sharon leaned forward in her seat, scanned the room with her deep-set cerulean eyes to make sure she had everyone's attention. She most certainly did.

She continued, "You all must your sex energy to increase your level of being. In the Work, there are seven levels of man. Every man is born either number one, number two, or number three. Man Number One is physical man, Man Number Two is emotional man, and Man

Number Three is intellectual man. You are all one of the above. They are all undesirable because you live in sleep and violence. But you are all luckily in School and in School—and only in School—can you possibly achieve the higher levels of Man. And this is only possible if you use your sex for the Work and your perfection. Man Number Four is balanced physically, intellectually, and emotionally. Man Number Five has self-consciousness and powers that an ordinary man does not possess. Man Number Six has objective consciousness and even more powers. Man Number Seven is the highest level—he has a soul and is immortal. People on this level include Christ, Buddha, Moses, Mohammed. I'm not on that level yet, but I'm very close and hope to be there soon."

Did she just say, "I'm very close?" I glanced over to Fred's face as these words left her lips. Not a squint, furrowed brow, or curl of the lip. Not a trace of disbelief. To the contrary, he looked ecstatic. So did Priscilla.

Sharon continued to speak for another hour or so. There was no interruption, and there were no questions asked by anyone. Sharon's perplexing, extraordinary boast sounded so delusional that it some-how had the opposite effect on me: it came off as self-confidence, authority. It was as if she possessed some magic, like she was letting us in on an important piece of wisdom especially for us. This woman had a certain power even though she seemed so grotesque; a visitor from a different School from another planet. She was frightening. If I'd seen her, say, sitting on a crowded subway next to an open seat, I wouldn't have taken it. Then she said it again, "Use your sex for the Work." Class ends.

At the next class, Fred and Priscilla announced to us that Sharon was their teacher. This was astonishing. We'd never realized that our teachers weren't at the top of the food chain. Fred asked to hear our impressions of Sharon. By and large the focus was on the shock that she was their teacher. Hardly anyone spoke about her directly except for Brian, a highly regarded trial lawyer who always seemed melancholy. He also had no filter or fear. He said, "Sharon was confusing. I couldn't follow her, and I was distracted by her nose job which seemed to be inconsistent with being a conscious being." Fred laced into Brian, "A lower level cannot recognize a higher level. You are on a lower level so you can't see Sharon. You need to work on yourself, Brian." Brian listened and thanked Fred. Fred didn't deny that Sharon had a nose job. Emma, Raymond, and a few others said that they wanted more material on the issue of "sex," but Fred said we would have to direct those questions to Sharon.

On her next visit a couple of weeks later, Sharon opened the class by inviting people to ask "questions about your being and the Work." Kim had been in School longer than the rest of the class and had an air of superiority. An attorney, she had once clerked for a United States Supreme Court Justice. She rose and asked Sharon for advice about her boyfriend and whether she should marry him. Sharon responded, "I don't tell people what to do. That's not what the Work is about. We can talk about what your Aims are, and we can talk about how you can use the Work as a lens to see your life." Sharon asked Kim questions about her boyfriend, what her hopes were, what her objections were. As Kim spoke, Sharon listened closely. Then she analyzed Kim's life, her upbringing, her past love affairs, and her boyfriend. The conversation lasted for about an hour. It was moving, uplifting, and emotional for Kim, and for me.

I got up the nerve to ask Sharon a question. I wanted to know more about the Work idea of "Internal Considering"—which means worrying about what people think about us—and I wanted to know how to use this idea to overcome self-consciousness. As I spoke, she fixed those cerulean eyes on me. It was the first time I experienced them. Her expression was focused, like a doctor carefully examining a wound or a professional basketball player about to take a free throw. She continued her penetrating gaze as she spoke, and said, knowingly, "Spencer, Internal Considering has held you back from getting what you want. It does this to everyone, but I know it has hurt you." *How did she know this?* I felt as if I were in a trance, under the care and protection of some divine benevolence. I sensed all sixty other students' eyes on me, their warmth. Their goodwill. She continued, "You have a big heart, so use it to 'Externally Consider' the other person by giving that person what they need and want and then you will not be focused on your own worries, insecurities, and fears. Use your heart. I know you can do this. Will you work on yourself?" I stared back at Sharon, said that I would, thanked her, and sat down. She nodded. This odd stranger's words had entered my heart, simultaneously frightening and delighting me. I was becoming more convinced than ever that School, that this Work—this mysterious source that filled me with wonder and awe—held the key to happiness, certainty, and order. Sharon possessed otherworldly influences. Which I wanted. I wanted the secret. I'd take that subway seat.

PART 3
1990–1999

Over the course of the next decade, School began to inhabit me in unexpected ways. I got involved in artistic and physical endeavors that I'd never tried before; I devoted substantial time and resources to recruiting for School; I traveled with School; I formed enduring relationships with other students and saw less of my "life friends" and family; I developed a deep relationship with Sharon, becoming part of her inner circle; I started a family; my mindset, my worldview, and my sense of myself began to conform with the Work's teachings. My private law practice flourished. My inner and outer lives began to merge with School. Certain of the secrets, mysteries, and intrigues of School were revealed and still more were presented—it was like for each revelation there were to be two more mysteries. I fell deeper under the spell of Sharon Gans.

Acting

Anti-fraternization rules are most common in the military, to maintain discipline and the chain of command. Banks don't allow tellers to mingle with customers for fear of fraud, and a divorce lawyer can get disbarred for bedding a client. Fred led us to believe that fraternizing blurred the distinction between life friendships and Essence friendships. But now, a year after coming to School, the rule was about to change.

When they relaxed the rule, we ran into each other's arms. The formality, the silence, the guilt over stolen glances, the suppression of hormones, the unnatural barrier—the Berlin Wall—were no more. Like a demolished dam floods the valley, the raging energy forever altered us—and Sharon. It led to deep friendships and relationships. It led to marriages. It led to families. It created a community. And it came suddenly, in a surprising way.

The catalyst was an "acting class like no other," as Fred described it to us. It was taught by one of Sharon's oldest friends, an actor named Joshua who we were told was not in School but a "friend of the Work." In the Spring of 1990, Sharon handpicked three dozen of her hundreds of students to attend. They were selected from three different classes: mine, the sustainers' class, and the Boston branch run by Robert. I was one of those picked. We were forbidden to discuss the existence of the acting class with the other students in our main

School class; it was secret class—a secret within a secret. In addition, we were not permitted to discuss School or anything about the Work during acting classes, even with the other students who were in School; and, of course, we were forbidden from speaking about School with the dozen acting students who were not in School at all. We were to meet twice a month on weekends in a loft on Lafayette Street across from the Public Theater. The cost was $100 per month.[6]

Joshua, who was in his early sixties like Sharon, had starred in a number of soap operas in the 1970s and 1980s, had supporting roles in several great films, and played a recurring role on a 1970s sitcom. Standing six feet tall with a large frame, combed-back wispy gray hair, a roundish face, and a large smile, he usually wore blue jeans and a polo shirt. During class, always in his hand was that iconic NYC take-out coffee cup with images of the Greek heroes. After class, when we all went out for drinks with him, he favored a stem glass with Absolut on the rocks. Thus, he usually smelled from either coffee or vodka, and always Old Spice. The opposite of Fred and the other teachers, he was personable, charming, approachable, and funny. It was love at first sight for me with Joshua. He sort of reminded me of my father.

His scene class was informal and fun. For the first time, fellow students from School could talk with each other outside class, mingle, practice scenes at each other's homes, speak by phone, and go for coffee, drinks, or dinner after acting class. After so many months of being prevented from the natural inclination to socialize (except for the few sanctioned planned activities outside class such as the square dancing and boat trips), coupled with the secret bond forged by School, deeper friendships formed quickly. In Joshua's class, we did scenes from every ilk of classic and contemporary plays and worked on improv. Some of the students were shooting to become professionals but mostly it was for fun. Eventually, Joshua started an improv

---

6   The anti-fraternization rule was changed a few months after the acting class began. Fred privately assembled the actors after class and told us that we could date anyone who attended the acting class, but not in the main class. It began a sort of feeding frenzy. Within a week, I went out on a date with someone from New York; and a few others from the Boston group called me asking to get together. Although the dates I had did not lead to anything serious, within a month, there were four serious couples from the acting class, two of whom got married within the next year.

show, and we performed a couple of times per month at the 13th Street Theater. I developed a lounge lizard character and performed it at cabarets. I even entered a contest called "New York's Funniest Lawyer" and won. I was having a blast.

Within several months, acting classes and performances became the center and focus of my social life. Joshua and my fellow acting classmates became my closest friends. My daily routine outside School was not much different now than it had been before. My new office was in Tribeca on Thomas Street. I had managed to attract enough clients to sustain my standard of living. I was still playing in the band with Joel, and I was dating women outside School. But the acting classes and performances were what I lived for. All the while, the Work and School were working profound changes on my identity.

On a winter evening I took the 6 train uptown to visit my old high school friend Vicki at her Upper East Side apartment. She had just given birth to her daughter, and she invited me up to meet her baby. I rang the bell and she led me into her living room. "Wait right here," she said. A moment later she reappeared from the bedroom walking slowly over to me with her infant, wrapped in a blanket. She carried this bundle like it was a sack of precious diamonds, close to her chest, careful not to drop a single stone. She handed me her treasure. It was a momentous occasion—my first childhood friend with a baby. But even as I held her daughter, I felt distant, disconnected, unattached to Vicki. Later, as I walked out into the cold night, I mulled over my lack of emotional response. The Work was pulling me away: acting class, the friendships, the ideas, all fusing in my psyche. As a student of the Work, I was headed in a distinct direction: to find the inner meanings of life and to evolve. People in life, including my life friends, were not interested in evolution—they were not interested in the invisible world. People in life, as we came to believe, were only interested in external things. We had nothing in common anymore except for history. It was bittersweet. The erosion of those friendships was replaced by the invisible power, protection, and support of the Work.

No notice was given when Sharon came to acting class one weekend. Some of the older male students hurriedly set up a comfortable chair, side table, and a vase with a rose of Sharon. She was helped into the chair. She wore her trademark flowing designer dress, fancy scarf, and her loud hair was in a top bun. A woman brought her a coffee and a snack plate. Joshua practically fell over himself too, making sure she was comfortable, affording her due deference. The atmosphere was suddenly formal, the actors tense and nervous, and Joshua's notes more severe. And then Sharon started to give notes to the actors and we learned that Sharon herself had been an actress! She mentioned that she had acted in the sixties with Joshua in groundbreaking experimental theater companies. In contrast to Joshua, she heaped praise on every scene and actor. She sprinkled her comments with references to Work terminology, such as Self-Remembering, Aim, and Internal Considering, as well as facts about people's personal lives. Sharon broke the fourth wall of the Work, the elephant in the room. But Sharon had the prerogative to do this, and we didn't. Emboldened, one of the students mentioned Self-Remembering, which elicited a glare from Sharon. His lack of discretion warranted his removal from class—we never saw him again in Joshua's class.

I had some unsettling interactions with Sharon and Robert at about this time.

Robert showed up one evening to see our improv show at the 13th Street Theater. Afterward I greeted him by name in the lobby, and he nodded his head. The next class he took me aside and scolded me for breaking the rule against invisibility, saying that I should not have spoken to him because people outside School were present and that it was highly "dangerous" for School and harmful for my evolution to be "casual about rules." I was struck by his intensity and anger and of course agreed that I had erred. I was being criticized for doing something that I'd had no idea was wrong. But like the incident with Hazel, in which I had to agree that I had lied when I hadn't, I accepted the tongue-lashing. What was different now was that I was more—much more—afraid. I was afraid that if I transgressed even once I might be thrown out of School. Exchanges like this with Robert were unnerving. But negative exchanges with Sharon were devastating. One stands out.

A few weeks later, Sharon came to an after-acting-class outing at a pub called The Stoned Crow near Washington Square Park. When it came time to leave, she asked me to walk her out to hail a cab. I was honored to be asked. As we walked alone together from the back room to the front door, I discreetly began to ask her for help on personal matters. She didn't answer. After we got outside and I had helped her up the stairs from the lower level to the street, she said to me, in disgust, "Spencer, you have no idea how to approach me as your teacher, and you better learn." I didn't know what she was referring to. I tried to retrace everything that I had done but couldn't think of anything egregious. It came out of left field and left me crestfallen. But I was sure I had done something. I must have. Being on her bad side was seriously risky business to me. I didn't want to take any risks.

Although Joshua was not a member of School, he had had a long friendship with Sharon and it was clear that he was familiar with Work ideas through their friendship; also, I had once noticed that he had Ouspensky's books in his apartment. So, the next day I asked Joshua about the exchange with Sharon. He said, "The way to evolve is to always ask yourself where you are at fault. That is the only way to take responsibility and gain understanding. Take full responsibility and change yourself." Joshua continued: "If someone walks up to you on the street and throws a pie in your face, you must ask yourself, 'What did I do to cause this to happen?'" This resonated—a way to understand any event by looking into my own thoughts, feelings, and actions. Maybe I could improve external events through my own actions. Maybe someone threw the pie at me, and not the person next to me, because he could sense that I was negative, or identified, or not remembering myself. After all, as Fred had said many times, other people can see us better than we see ourselves. The pie thrower was doing me a favor. There is nothing random in this ordered universe. I thanked Joshua for his insights. I came back to this pearl of wisdom for many years. It shaped my thinking and reaction to events for decades. It helped me to accept and welcome and embrace Sharon's and other teachers' actions as guidance. It seemed like a spiritual awakening, another piece to the puzzle of truth, toward freedom.

Third Line of Work

After a year of being in School, about half of the students in our class were pulled aside one night after class and asked to recruit new students. By then we had gained affection for School and understanding of the Work ideas. Recruiting was presented as both a privilege and an obligation and those of us selected were to consider it a distinction; that we were somehow more advanced than the thirty other students who were not asked to do recruiting. It was also presented as a means to help us better value the Work. It was an honor—we were deemed "ready" to "ascend the ladder" by putting new people in our place. Hierarchy was a very important part of the Work. As spelled out by Sharon, consciousness was graded on a scale from one to seven, and we all wanted to move up, move up to the level of a Christ, Moses, Plato, or Buddha. As for the obligation, it was part of the bargain of School. Fred told us, "The Work has given you so much and now it's time to give back to School. And while you are benefiting School, you will be benefiting yourself and the World. Most importantly, you will be giving an enormous gift to some lucky individual. Don't forget how much you have benefited." Fred and Sharon did not invent this: Gurdjieff himself did. According to Gurdjieff, in a real School students must be working on "Three Lines of Work."

1. The "First Line of Work" is 100 percent for you personally. This is your personal work—the self-observation exercises, trying to remember yourself, trying not to identify and so on.

2. "Second Line of Work" is where you help your neighbor—in this case other students—to work on themselves while also saying to yourself whatever you say to them: in this way Second Line of Work is 50 percent for the other and 50 percent for you.

3. "Third Line of Work" is where you give 100 percent to School—to keep it functioning and maintained in all respects. Gurdjieff insisted that engaging in Third Line of Work helped the other Lines of Work and that by not doing Third Line of Work individual evolution was impossible. The cornerstone of Third Line of Work was to recruit new students.

When Bruce and Heather were recruiting me, it was almost as if they were following some sort of script or playbook in terms of what and how they said things to entice me. And indeed there was—a sophisticated method developed and perfected over the course of many years by Sharon. The point of the system was to simultaneously lure and vet candidates while also keeping the process entirely secret so that only the best candidates ever found out about the existence of School. We were given detailed training on how to recruit and I took notes. Let's call it the "Recruitment Manual."

The Recruitment Manual

I. Fishing for Men and Women: Qualified Candidates
    *   Men or women between 25 and 40. This is the prime age for someone to come to School. They are already somewhat established in life but are not crystalized or set in ways which are hard to change.

- Gainfully employed earning at least $100,000 annually.[7] Someone coming into School must be a "Good Householder"—i.e., that they can pay their own way and afford School. Unless a person is willing to pay for something, he does not value it. Therefore, payment is essential to value one's evolution. No losers allowed.
- Neither candidate nor any immediate family member may be employed as a journalist, author, or in any kind of law enforcement. These people tend to be curious or nosy by nature and it could pose a risk to the invisibility of School. If someone wrote about School, it would kill it.
- Nobody in therapy. Nobody who takes drugs. Nobody who is disabled. These people are damaged goods. Sharon does not have the energy to help them.
- Candidates must be white and straight. As Sharon once put it, "People of color[8] and gay people tend to have a 'chip on their shoulder' and are skeptical and unwilling to be open to the Work." Although in some cases a gay person will be considered if they are open minded to being converted to a straight life and get married to someone in class of the opposite sex.
- Candidates cannot be living with any parent or sibling.
- Candidates must be "disappointed" in their life or at a crossroads and looking for answers. This is probably the most crucial qualification. The candidate needs to be unhappy or dissatisfied about something important in their life and looking for answers, meaning, and help. Not despairing, but disappointed: empty.
- Candidates should not already be involved in religious, spiritual, or other groups. We want to be their prime place for spirituality. The Work is a jealous mistress. No dabblers.

---

7   This figure is adjusted by inflation to account for the value in the early 1990s.

8   Sometime after I left School, I shared this rule with my Jamaican friend Lydia. She laughed and explained that "no black person would be dumb enough to go to a secret meeting of a group of white people."

- While it's preferable to recruit single candidates, because spouses are nosy, a married candidate is acceptable so long as the candidate demonstrates that they have some measure of independence from the spouse for attending classes twice a week. It is also allowable and possible to bring a married couple to the Work.
- Do not have any conjugal relations with the candidate, without prior permission from Sharon.[9] Still, if your candidate is of the opposite sex, use your sex energy to entice them. It's OK if the candidate likes you but don't act like you are going on "serious" dates. Do not expressly lead them on, otherwise they may be disappointed when you introduce them to School.

II. Where to Fish: Rules of Engagement
- Go on outings to find candidates at least seven times per week. Go to places like museums, the theater, dance performances, concerts, libraries, or any other cultural places and innocently strike up conversations with strangers with the Aim of recruiting them. Dress nicely. Remember you are a representative of the Work.
- When not on specific outings and over the course of your usual day, strike up at least ten conversations per day with strangers—in subways, coffee shops, streets, bookshops, bars, Bloomingdale's, the opera, an airplane, the supermarket, etc. Ask provocative questions: "Who are our heroes today?" "What is the meaning of life?" "Do you think there is an invisible world?"
- Be positive and show great interest in the other person. Try to steer conversations toward seeing what this person's worldview is like to both glean their perspective

---

9   Unless one was in acting class and wanted to date someone who was also in acting class, prior explicit permission needed to be obtained from Sharon to date anyone in School. And even if one chose to date a fellow actor, Sharon needed to be informed. In some instances, she disapproved of acting couples and terminated those relations.

and pique their interest. Compliment and flatter. Listen to them.

- Get their phone numbers, but only give them your service number. Do not give them your last name. If they ask, give a fake one. Call from a blocked phone.

III. The Bait: The First Three Meetings

NB: Never mention the words School or the Work until you receive permission from Hazel. [Although she was not a teacher, Hazel headed up recruiting and was considered an older student in a leadership role.] *Also, it is entirely possible to combine many meetings into one or two if you have a great candidate and have gotten permission from Hazel.*[10]

- The First Meeting, like all of them, should be held in a public place over coffee, a meal, even the park. The first meeting is an open-ended conversation to talk about the state of the world. Everything and anything about politics, history, society in order to get a sense of your candidate's worldview. Make them feel special and interesting. Listen to them. Compliment and flatter. People love it.

- The Second Meeting is for "qualifying" your candidate. Check the boxes. Find out their income, their work history, their family's occupations, their sexual preferences,[11] and all the other things listed above in part I. Write up a detailed dossier on your candidate and hand it in to Hazel.

- The Third Meeting is for finding out your candidate's ache: are they looking for something else in life besides just making money and getting married? Do they have a desire to change themselves? What is the meaning of their

---

10 Bruce was having such trouble getting me to meetings that he was allowed to expedite the process. He joked with me that I had been a "difficult fish to reel in" and told me that Hazel was guiding him every step of the way (including telling him to show up at my band recording).

11 Sharon believed and stated that homosexuality was a choice, and a bad one at that. She claimed LGBTQ people were "passive."

life? Can they appreciate the invisible world? Do they have an itch? Can you picture them in School?

- In the Second and Third Meetings, start planting seeds about Schools—i.e., that they existed throughout civilization to help mankind attain consciousness and obtain their goals, etc. If they like theater, tell them Shakespeare was in a School; if they are Christian tell them Jesus was in a School; if they like music tell them Bach was in a School; etc.

- Remember, you want to find people who are disappointed or at a crossroads. You want people who are looking for friends. We don't want loners or losers or depressive people. Think about where you were when you met the Work.

- Find out what has kept them from getting what they want in life. They will love you for asking. Put yourself in their shoes.

- During all meetings, talk about Work ideas that might be of interest to them (but don't use Work terminology). See how they react. You want them to think you have something of value. It would be ideal if they ask things like, "How interesting. How do you know this?" You will answer by saying something like, "Well, I've been studying for a long time. And I have amazing friends." When they ask for details just say that you will tell them once you get to know them better.

- Also, find a way to say to them, "I used to think like that but now I think differently." This will be provocative in a good way. And it will make them think you have something. You want them to look up to you.

IV. Getting Help with Fishing: Meetings with Leaders
- The thirty recruiters are assigned into one of six groups of five students. Each group is assigned a leader—an older student who knows the ropes.[12]

---

12 Both Bruce and Heather were group leaders and were considered the best recruiters in School.

- Recruiters are to meet after every class for an hour or more to discuss all our candidates with Hazel and each of the group leaders. (The after-class meetings could go on until 2:00 a.m., and these were workdays.)
- Each candidate will be discussed collectively so that everyone can see how everyone else is doing: what people are doing right and what people are doing wrong. Yes, there is a competition among you students to have the most candidates: S says competition is good for inner development. You want to be a winner, not a loser.
- We will discuss all the personal details of every candidate as a group and brainstorm on how to get the candidate interested in School and how to weed out candidates who are not good fits. This is the place to ask for help and to get it.
- You need to call your group leader twice a day to give a report and get help.
- In addition to the meetings immediately following class, we will meet at the Gemini Coffee Shop on the corner of East Thirty-fifth Street and Second Avenue at 6:00 a.m. every Friday morning to discuss our Aims and our results. Fred may show up by surprise occasionally. Consider these meetings like class. Be on time.
- On Saturday nights, you will meet with your group leader and group for dinner to discuss your Aims and results. After dinner, you are to take off the rest of the evening and not do any recruiting; it is to be like the Sabbath. Everyone needs a day off to rest, even God. On Sundays, you will have "flash meetings" where you will meet with your group at landmark locations (such as the steps of the New York City Public Library, the Museum of Modern Art, Lincoln Center) and then go out in pairs to find new people. These meetings will give you energy and support because you will be working directly with your classmates.

V. Keeper or Dud: The Fourth Meeting
- The Fourth Meeting is where a group leader joins you and your candidate at a meeting. At this meeting, the candidate can be further assessed, and a decision can be made afterward as to whether to invite.
- Invite a group leader of the candidate's opposite sex. Group leaders know how to seduce a candidate with the sex energy of the Work.
- During the meeting, display your invisible, special connection with your group leader. Make the candidate yearn to have a relationship like yours. Pull out all the stops.
- If a decision is made to invite, you will hold a Fifth Meeting. Most candidates never get this far. Congratulations.

VI. Reeling in the Fish: The Fifth Meeting
- Tell the candidate that you have a secret you've never told a soul and get them to agree to maintain the secret.
- Explain to them that this offer is very special, rare, and an unusual opportunity. And only open for a short time.
- Explain to them that this is a real esoteric school connected to a tradition of knowledge, but that it's not for everyone.
- Tell them about how it has helped you, how you have wonderful deep friendships, and that the teachers are special.
- Explain that there is a one-month free experiment to commit to but afterward there is monthly tuition.
- If they are interested, schedule a sixth meeting with a teacher.

VII. The Sixth Meeting
- This is with a teacher. If your candidate has been properly prepared this will be a joy, a time to celebrate.
- Most candidates come nervous, but Fred and Robert and the others know what they are doing. Watch, enjoy, celebrate. Congratulations. You have changed their lives, changed yours, and changed School.

During a Saturday-afternoon blizzard in January 1991, I bundled up and trudged out from my apartment in the Village, taking the empty 6 train up to the Metropolitan Museum of Art. I emerged from the staircase into a world of white. It was snowing so hard that the shovelers had all but given up clearing the stone stairs leading from Fifth Avenue to the Beaux-Arts entrance. I'd come here twice weekly for almost a year. I entered through the revolving doors and came into the Great Hall, which no longer felt great. I paid my ten dollars, fastened the tiny red metal button on my winter coat, and went up to my usual spot.

Standing in the small puddle my rubber boots left on the marble floor, I pretended to contemplate Rembrandt's *Aristotle Contemplating the Bust of Homer*. I was here on a secret mission for the welfare of the planet. The continuation of School was an imperative for civilization to exist, and civilization wouldn't exist unless new members were recruited. It had to be done with stealth to protect School, myself, and potential students. My classmates and I had been working on recruitment for nine months. About half a dozen of my classmates—having been unable to weather the round-the-clock work required to recruit—either stopped recruiting or left School entirely. The line of Work would end on Wednesday. Finally. I had not yet brought a single person to School.

I had a plan. I would wait for someone to look at the painting. The ideal target would be someone in their late twenties to mid-thirties. Man or woman—didn't matter. I would size them up. Their clothing, their body language, their "vibrations." If they didn't emanate an offensive body odor or mumble to themselves, I'd begin my approach. I would sort of sidle up next to them, just close enough to be heard with a museum whisper. When the moment was right, I would turn and say, in a soft voice of wonder, "It's breathtaking, isn't it? Did you ever wonder how on earth he could do this?" The purpose of this question was to initiate a discussion which would ideally unfold as follows:

Target [*thirty-five-year-old man*]: I was thinking the same thing. I don't know. What do you think?

Me [*chumming the waters*]: Rembrandt was a genius, and he also had the help of conscious men and women.

Target [*sniffing at it*]: What do you mean by conscious men and women?

Me [*dangle but not time to reel in; be vague*]: I'll put it this way: people who believed that we were put here on this planet to do more than just go to work, have families, go to church, and then die.

Target [*nibbling*]: Interesting. How do you know about this? Are you some sort of historian?

Me [*reel him in with the classic line*]: Well, I've been very lucky. I study very hard, and I have special, wonderful friends. My name is Spencer, what is yours? [*extending my hand*]

Target [*pulling this fish into the fucking boat—YESS!!*]: Nice to meet you, Spencer, I'm Kevin. What is it that you study? Who are your friends?

Me [*confidentially*]: Well, it's not something I usually speak about, but if you want, when I get to know you better, I can tell you more about it. Tell you what, if you want to grab a bite with me, I can bring a friend and maybe we can talk more?

Target: That would be great. When?

Me: Kevin, I'm curious, what do you do for a living? [*We need to do some screening: no cops, journalists, vagabonds, or ne'er do wells.*]

Target: Oh, I'm retired [*bingo*]. I used to work on Wall Street, now I live on a farm in Westchester with my family, but I keep an apartment in NYC [*good, he has some independence*] which is near my woodworking shop. [*This keeps getting better: School needs people who are good for construction projects.*] What do you do, Spencer?

Me: Oh, I'm a lawyer. [*Looking at my watch*] I'm sorry, Kevin, to be abrupt but I have to head out. [*I don't, but I want to keep him hanging. Because he is such a good candidate, I am going to bring this directly to a Fourth Meeting.*] Let's have dinner tomorrow night, OK? And I will bring a friend.

Target: Sure, my number is 111-5555. 7:00 p.m. works.

Me: Let's go to the Blue Water Grill on Union Square.

In reality, on this day, I encountered thus with my question about how on earth Rembrandt created this masterpiece: (a) a petite young woman with dark black hair smiling and telling me in an Eastern Europe accent that she didn't speak English; (b) a bearded heavy-set man in his mid-thirties wearing a bottle-green ski parka who smirked and said, "He used paint" as he walked away; and (c) two young women who giggled and quickly walked away holding hands. On only one occasion did a target engage with me for a few minutes until he claimed that Rembrandt was really a "Jew," and that "they ran the world."

I forged on. I owed School. I wanted to evolve. Plus, it was mandatory, or we'd be forced to leave, we were told. We were castigated for poor results. "Your valuation is off, and you are not showing gratitude to Sharon and the Work." I was trying to work against Internal Considering. I had approached strangers in mid-day in midtown and at night in NoHo and asked them who their heroes were. Hoping for answers like Odysseus, strangers (if they even spoke to me) would say things like Norman Schwarzkopf, Lou Reed, or "fuck off, creep." I would frequent downtown places like Old Towne Bar, McSorley's Old Ale House, Estancia 460, the Odeon, and Pete's Tavern, get a drink, and ask people about the "meaning of life" only to be met with reactions ranging from amusement (a group of frat boys taunted me) to fear (a young lady called over the bartender). I'd go to bookstores like Barnes & Noble or the Academy and ask people who were minding their own business to tell me about the book they were looking at. It was a desperate nine months.

I didn't recruit anyone, but I did have my ATM card stolen by a charming young woman whom I met at Fraunces Tavern. I had several meetings with a contractor named Steve who interpreted my interest as romantic and was hurt when I invited him to "the month's experiment." I didn't recognize the actor Bruno Kirby when I started chatting him up at Barneys but realized after the fact. He was polite and friendly, but he was not interested in getting together to "discuss the state of the world."

When Wednesday rolled around, Fred held a meeting after class with the thirty of us who had spent the last nine months on Third Line of Work. We had managed to bring a total of ten new people, of whom only six or so stayed beyond a month. Fred told us it was a great success. He said we had grown our beings.[13]

---

13 We continued to perform Third Line of Work numerous other times for extended periods. In addition to the method described above, we once mounted lecture series open to the public which were secretly recruitment events. They were held at a theater on East 17th Street on Union Square and hundreds attended. The series was called "Searching for Meaning," with lectures given by students on such topics as "Making Plato Practical" and "Butterflies and Evolution" and "Time Travel." We were all to attend and recruit from the audience during intermission, as well as before and after the lectures.

Have You Made Your Aim?

Every four weeks was "Aim Night." One at a time, each student would stand in succession and solemnly state their Aim—a four-week project or goal that we would work on outside class. "My Aim is to take two archery classes per week and practice three hours per week." "My Aim is to read *The Three Musketeers*." "My Aim is to take two classical guitar lessons a week and practice an hour a day." "My Aim is to write one poem a day." "My Aim is to keep track of every dollar I spend." "My Aim is to go on at least two dates per week with new people I've never met before." "My Aim is to cook dinner at home at least three times per week." On the following Aim Night, we would state whether we completed our Aims. We were to use the "force of the Work and its ideas" to help us accomplish them. This was an opportunity to make the Work ideas practical as well as to get the hang of what it meant to follow through on a commitment and be accountable to our classmates. Also, our sustainers would check in with us to help us along and achieve our Aims.

The obstacles to meeting our Aims were called "intervals," which occurred, by law, in every single endeavor. But by Self-Remembering at each interval a person could cross the interval and complete the Aim and not digress or "miss the mark." As Fred put it, the critical aspect of Aim was that without School and its hidden ancient knowledge, one could not achieve a goal with consciousness and would run a high risk of not achieving it at all. "Sleeping Humanity" (i.e., anyone not in School) would lie to themselves, justifying their failures and settling for mediocrity rather than having the tools (e.g., Self-Remembering) to succeed. Fred had given us the example of the person who set out to be an artist but ended up in disappointment and disillusionment getting a job as an accountant and giving up his art.

Exactly four weeks after we started our Aims, Fred would begin class by asking, "Who made their Aim?" We would applaud those of us who stood and would show concern at those who didn't. That's because we were a microcosmos, and if one person didn't make their Aim, none of us did. It was a failure, and our friends let us down. And to some degree we let them down for not helping them make their Aim. Fred would ask the non-standers individually why they didn't make their Aim—it was always the case that they were either not working on themselves or not asking for help. "It's all for learning," Fred would explain after each allocution. This was a good incentive to make your Aim. But for those who did make it, they would give reports or, in some cases, presentations on their experiences. (For example, we would be entertained by our classmates performing stand-up comedy, tango, and beginner's classical guitar.) Those evenings gave us a collective and personal sense of accomplishment—assuming everyone stood—and a certain gratitude to School for the experiences we had.

There was a student named Harvey who was a diamond dealer, dad of two, and husband of Marion, another student. He walked with a cane, and they were among the wealthiest couples in School. He was feisty and liked to challenge Fred. One night, he stood up and asked, "Is School really necessary to accomplish an Aim? They landed a human on the moon, split the atom, and cured so many diseases without School." I was thinking the same thing. I was so glad I didn't ask. Fred took a long pause—he lowered his head as though in a prayer, then looked out across the room in silence—this was about thirty seconds long and seemed like forever. (He once did the "Fred

Pause" for fifteen minutes.) Then he had gathered himself, and spoke calmly, to the entire class, with the conviction of a prosecutor making his closing statement.

"It's always a question of sincerity, Harvey. We don't have a permanent or unchangeable I. There are millions of separate small I's. One moment we can be kind and the next murderous. It's like a person with multiple personalities. And this is us. This is our predicament." I'd heard Fred's spiel about multiplicity a bazillion times, but it always rang true. "In the Work, we seek to become unified by getting in touch with the I's in us that are interested in the Work, that like the Work, that are receptive to the Work. These are called 'Work I's.'" His insistence on unity made anything less than perfection an abject failure. This fundamental concept was dogma for us all. "Life I's on the other hand hate the Work and are ill-informed, cynical, and violent. They want to kill the Work and kill us. So, to evolve we must cultivate Work I's. And you can only do this in School and with the help of teachers and friends. Work I's eventually lead to 'Real Will.' It is said in the Work that we have many lifetimes and that even if we are lucky to find School in our next lifetime, it can take many lifetimes to build a soul. Only a handful of men have done this: Christ, Buddha, and the like. Sharon is very close to this level. But we as her students can try to come from Work I's and we can do this by remembering ourselves."

Now Fred came back to Harvey. "When you make statements or pose questions in class—as I say—it's a matter of sincerity, and from which I's you are speaking from. Ask yourself where you are coming from when you speak—Work I's (which are open to the Work) or Life I's which want to kill it and kill you and kill Sharon. What's behind your question? What's the motive? Is it to learn and to try to become a good student of the Work? Or is there an ulterior motive?" Fred then opened a copy of *The Psychology of Man's Possible Evolution* and read from Ouspensky's introduction where he criticizes attendees of his lectures, saying that they didn't listen to the lectures to hear something new:

They did not formulate it for themselves, but in fact they always tried to contradict this in their minds and translate what they heard into their habitual language, whatever it happened to be.

I know that it is not an easy thing to realize that one is hearing new things. We are so accustomed to the old tunes, and the old motives, that long ago we ceased to hope and ceased to believe that there might be anything new. I cannot guarantee that you will hear new ideas, that is, ideas you never heard before, from the start; but if you are patient, you will very soon begin to notice them. And then I wish you not to miss them, and to try not to interpret them in the old way.

Fred paused. We were in a deep state of contemplation, nodding our heads in agreement. Harvey was missing an important point. Something new was being said. Fred wanted us not to miss it. He was trying to help us. The concept of Aim was central—pivotal—to my connection with School. Aim gave me the conviction that I could gain the ability to control events. Fred continued:

"Landing a man on the moon was not a conscious act. It did not come from School. It was an Aim set by life. And what did it achieve? Nothing. Some rocks? Tang? Publicity? Splitting the atom was one of the worst, most violent things man has done. Einstein had an outsized intellectual center but lacked any humanity. As for curing diseases, most of these cures were accidents: scientists and investors test different potions, and they have no idea what they are doing. These are accidents—not Aims." Fred delivered this with passion, brimming with confidence with a dose of irony and sarcasm. He gesticulated wildly, his eyes twitching, and his white hair seeming aglow. His passion had a stirring effect on the room. It was all part of the education School dispensed, not unlike a tough drill sergeant or trainer whose techniques seemed harsh but who only wanted the best for their trainees—the tougher it was, the better it was. I found myself going into a sort of hazy place where I wasn't so much thinking as *absorbing*. Fred's mouth making shapes in the air before me, his nasal voice blending with the atmosphere in the room. I went into a "Fred Trance." His conviction solidified, deepened my appreciation of Aim.

My and my classmates' lives outside School at this time were just like any New Yorker's.

I went to my office every morning, downtown in Tribeca. I worked in a loft on Thomas Street. I'd take the 2 or 3 train from my apartment on Fifth Avenue and Twelfth Street around 8:30 a.m. I shared the office with Joel and three other lawyers. A commercial litigator, I tried business cases: disputes between companies ranging from breach of contract to partnership disputes to intellectual property to real estate cases. For a couple of years, I also represented indigents facing criminal charges as a part-time public defender. After work I would usually come home and make dinner or order in Chinese food from the Cottage on Christopher Street or hamburgers or diner food from Joe Juniors on Sixth Avenue. On Fridays, the guys in my office would head down to the Odeon for drinks and try to pick up women at the bar. I still smoked about two and a half packs of cigarettes a day. I never worked out. At Morton's suggestion, I bought a car and went out of town on weekends, sometimes going with friends to ski upstate or to the beach in the summer.

Although I continued to remain close with my mother and Matthew—and we saw each other on holidays and other occasions—these relationships began to change, and I saw less of them and spoke less to them. They didn't know about my involvement in School: I never mentioned it to anyone. But my family was "in life," and therefore could not possibly be interested in the inner meanings of life and personal evolution. I was now closer with my School friends, my Essence friends who were by definition closer than my biological family. I would sooner confide with School friends about things I had previously only told my family. Sharon or Fred wanted us to start to keep our families at arm's length. Sharon used to paraphrase (and misuse) Christ's injunction to: "hate his own father and mother and wife and children and brothers and sisters." She said that one needed

to separate from one's family to become real students of the Work.
Later, she told me—and several men in class—that we didn't want to
become "momma's boys" and should only speak with our mothers on
their birthdays and Mother's Day.

Sharon Nights, Part I

Sharon began attending classes more regularly, although we were never sure when she was coming until the moment we were seated silently in class and two men walked to the front of the room carrying her foot-high wooden platform. Some students held their breath. Some shut their eyes, nodding their heads solemnly as is if to say, "Thank you, Lord." Others looked down at their laps. I felt butterflies. Once the heavy platform was slowly lowered to the wooden floor, two other men would carefully place upon it her leather recliner; another man would place the side table; a woman would place upon the table a plate of prosciutto, fontina, and figs and a place setting; a fifth man would place Sharon's Absolut on the rocks in a stem glass along with an ashtray and a pack of Marlboro Light 100s; and finally a second woman would place the vase with a rose of Sharon. It was considered an honor for these students to perform these tasks for Sharon's arrival (it was called "Teachers' Service") and everyone who watched was a little jealous of them.

Tonight, Sharon's platform was set up but alongside it there were three—not the usual two—empty teacher seats. We waited in silence, reading, smoking cigarettes, or meditating. And then Sharon, along with Fred and Maude, entered from the back of the room as we students stood to greet them.

"Where is Kim?" Sharon asked loudly as she was helped up to her recliner by Fred. Kim remained standing, "I'm here, Sharon, hello!" "Good, Kim, come up here and sit next to me." Kim rushed up to the empty seat to Sharon's right as Fred and Maude sat to her left. Sharon smiled, started to applaud, and yelled, "Congratulations, Kim, on your engagement!" At that moment, several women entered from the back room holding balloons, trays of sixty glasses of champagne, and a dozen wrapped gifts. We all applauded and hooted.

When we settled down, Sharon said, "Kim, you took the help that the Work gave you about your fiancé—the Work works." Kim was in tears, overwhelmed. We made toasts—speeches—she opened her gifts, she cried more. And finally she spoke about how grateful she was for the help Sharon had given her life. It was inspiring and emotional. One could sense the hope in the room.

After about an hour of celebrating, a woman named Karla stood up. "Sharon, I need your help. I love my husband; we have a beautiful family and a good marriage. But I have been having fantasies about being with other men. I don't want to cheat but I cannot stop this fantasy. It's driving me a little crazy. How do I stop this? What would the Work say?"

Sharon responded, "The Work is also called the way of the sly man. We live in life but with a secret. And we work with Aim. Why not have it all, Karla? You are beautiful. Go to Italy. Visit the museums. Visit the Spanish Steps. Stand at the fountain. Wait for a man. Have an affair. Come back. Remember yourself." Karla was now a shade of purple. Sharon asked, "How does this help feel, Karla?"

Karla responded, "I couldn't possibly do that." Sharon said.

"First of all, how would he ever know?" Karla said.

"That's not the problem, Sharon; it's adultery, and it's lying."

Sharon got testy, "Morality is a false and artificial phenomenon. It's based on superstition and fear. Give it up, Karla. Be free. There is such a thing as 'Clever Insincerity'—say and do whatever is necessary to achieve your Aim. If your fantasy is to have another man, then go have fun and don't be insincere with yourself." The class was nodding in agreement. I thought it was totally nuts and counterproductive, but it also seemed so wild and uninhibited and appealing. Apparently,

Karla felt the same way, because she did go to Italy and met a guy at the Spanish Steps, and they had an affair.

Eric was a Wall Street broker. Handsome, smart, and charming, he was one of Sharon's favorite students. On this night, he announced that he had received a bonus of $20,000 from his company for being the employee of the month. The class erupted in applause. Eric said that he was grateful to the Work because without the "force" of School he would not have gotten it. Sharon praised him and said, "The best way to thank the Work is not in words, but in deeds—you must give back to School with interest otherwise you lose its force." Eric understood what was being said. Shortly after class, he wrote out a check for $20,000 to Sharon.

Lace on the Gloves

As directed, one Friday night in the winter of 1991, I took the subway to the High Street stop in downtown Brooklyn and walked over to a deserted section with old warehouses on the river. It was a dark and sketchy area, made more unnerving by broken streetlights and the heartbreaking sight of a man wearing a Hefty bag as a shawl, shuffling past, and talking to himself. I found the address and saw some of my classmates waiting in the lobby of a warehouse. We got in the creaky elevator and went to the third floor. I still didn't know where we were headed. As the elevator door slowly slid open, I could hear the activity of a gym—fast movements, grunting—and I could smell years of body odor wafting into the elevator. The door opened completely to an entire floor of an old boxing gym. There were five rings. The place hadn't been painted or swept since 1953. This was the legendary Gleason's Gym. And the famous quote from the Aeneid of Virgil was painted on the wall: "*Now whoever has courage and a strong and collected spirit in his breast, let him come forward, lace on the gloves and put up his hands.*" Men were in the rings sparring. Men were pummeling body bags and speed bags that lined the huge room. There were coaches, assistants, and other boxers waiting to get in the rings. The lighting was bright, and everything echoed in the huge place. The stench, the noise, the lights, and the hectic energy were thrilling.

My sustainer, Morton, was there along with one other man I recognized from the older class, Karl, who was a master carpenter. Morton said that we must not talk about Work ideas in front of anyone at the gym, including our boxing instructors, Junior and José, his son. This was the first we knew why we had come to this address—to box. We were introduced to another student named Glen, a doctor, who announced that he was going to be leading the "Line of Work." He explained to us that we would be working under internal Aims and that we would need to have a new one for each night we met (we would meet weekly every Friday evening plus one Saturday morning per month). We would state our Aims to Morton or Karl and work with them throughout the evening. We would then be arranged into groups and work with the trainers and also with Morton and Karl who would suit up and train with us as well. We would be sparring. Unlike other School revelations (and rules), this involved my body, my physical well-being. It was invasive. I had conflicting feelings. I resented the pressure to do something I didn't want to do and felt guilt for wanting to resist.

And yet it was also a new world I wanted to learn. In our first lesson we learned the basics of the boxing stance: foot placement, body placement, hand placement, and how to move around the ring. We learned the basics of throwing a punch—it's a quick motion, like grabbing a coin. I now saw my classmates in a different light. The pecking order shifted. The stronger, taller, heavier men were now looked at differently: with respect, irrespective of whether they were favorites of Sharon. After the workout, we met at a restaurant under the Brooklyn Bridge, the twenty-four of us led to a back room filled with several tables pushed together. Fred was there. He spoke to us. He was smiling from ear to ear.

"You will learn things about yourself and your fellow men from this Line of Work that you can never learn in any other way. That's because you will not only learn how to box, which in and of itself is a remarkable sport on so many levels, but mostly because you will be using the Work ideas to engage in this sport. The Aim is not to become good boxers, it's to become men in the Work sense.

You don't realize how strong you are. You have no idea. There are so many principles that you will come up against in this sport, in going to combat—how to 'run with your fear,' how to give and take a 'punch with love,' what it means to be courageous and a hero, how to go against your False Personality, how to practice relaxation when being punched, how to practice Non-Identification, and how to remember yourself."

We went around the table and each man spoke about their experience. Aside from a couple of us, nobody had ever boxed, but within a month, we were ready to spar.

My first time sparring in the ring was with Morton. Although he was slightly taller than me, I was stronger and heavier than him. I was going to fucking kill this poor skinny Ivy League nebbish. We got in the center of the ring and touched gloves. The lights were hot, and the room echoed with grunts, snapping speed bags, and thudding body bags. I was pumped. Morton and I backed away in our postures, dancing and guarding. I was thinking that if I hit him too hard, I'd kill him. So, I figured that the best thing would be to play defense, land a few body jabs, and then do him in, but politely. While I was formulating this plan in my head, Morton's brown glove landed like a speeding brick square on my nose. I heard the crunch, a crack. I saw stars. My head reeled. He backed off and smirked. I looked down on my brown gloves, which were now wet with blood. I shouted, "What was that?" Morton said, "You were not guarding. This is what happens." I screamed, "Fuck you. What the hell are you talking about?" Glen suddenly appeared in the ring and handed me a towel: "Sit down, buddy. Hold this on your nose. Are you feeling light-headed, dizzy?" I told him I was. He said, "I know it hurts, but you will be OK. Try not to react now. Observe yourself and remember your Aim. What is your Aim?" I said, "Are you kidding?" He said he wasn't and pressed me. I said, "To practice relaxation." He smiled, patted me on the back, and said, "That's a perfect Aim. You can do that now. Let's get out of the ring and you can wash up." I told Glen that I wanted to go to the ER because I thought I broke my nose or had had a concussion. He told me not to go and that I was just shaken up. Inasmuch as he was a doctor and leading the Line of Work, I listened to him. I never sought medical advice.[14]

At dinner, seeing that almost everyone else got knocked around by more experienced boxers and having decided to "speak from the Work," I reported, "I learned a lot from that punch. I learned that I need to always be vigilant and remember my Aim. If I had been practicing relaxation and had not been tight and afraid, I would have been able to block that punch or at least not feel the pain as much as I had. Also I wish I hadn't been afraid to hurt him." Glen told me this was great work. He also told me that this was an opportunity to practice non-identification with my body. "You are not your body; you are not your bloody nose. When you can do this, you are also not identified with the body's pain." Remembering Joshua's pie thrower, I thanked Morton for punching me so hard and helping me to be awake. My classmate Donald, who was married to a wealthy widow who was another student, complimented me on seeing all these things and said that I was lucky to have taken this punch. Sidney chimed in that this punch was thrown with "love" and that was because Morton wanted me to learn something from this. I thanked Sidney and Donald. I felt the love.

School supplied endless intrigue and shocks. We loved the surprise fishing trip, the surprise acting class, and boxing. We loved that Sharon seemed to know so many things about our life—like she was a mind reader, and so was Fred. It seemed like magic. And here was another shock: Glen announced to us that we were going to have boxing matches against each other—three rounds of one minute each.

When we arrived at the gym, Glen told us who we would be fighting. I was matched up to fight Edgar. He was a good ten years older than me, and about my size. And now another stunner: streaming in were all the other men and women in the class, along with Sharon and Fred. Another man also entered with them: he was tall, broad, with gray hair and eyebrows as bushy as a squirrel's tail. I rec-

---

14 My broken nose was one of several such injuries. Although we did wear head guards, that did not stop us from getting concussions. I don't remember anybody ever going to an emergency room or doctor during the sessions.

ognized him because he had once walked into Joshua's acting class to drop off Sharon. It was Alex Horn, Sharon's husband. They took seats around the main ring, evidently to watch our match. The men were shocked to see Sharon and further baffled by the attendance of Alex, whom most of us had never laid eyes on before.

Mine was the eighth fight out of ten. The first fight was between Joey and Sean. They were of equal height—about five feet, seven inches—and had small frames. Sean was particularly thin. But they were both excellent boxers. They entered the ring with the entire class watching. I stood off to the side with some of the other men. We felt lucky we weren't going first. We were pumped and we were tense. Glen reminded us to "work on yourselves and remember your aims."

Joey and Sean met in the center and touched gloves before being sent to their corners. The bell rang. The two ran toward each other and a flurry of wild punches were thrown. It looked like a wild street fight. The months of meticulous training on the form and the technique and the art of boxing went out the window of a speeding car. This was a savage battle to the death. Nobody had expected this. Apparently, the live audience, the presence of classmates, teachers, Sharon and Alex, got to Joey and Sean; they'd transformed into psychotic gladiators looking to kill each other with maximum mayhem. When the first round was over, they returned to their corners and rested. Sean's face was crimson. Joey's eyes were glazed. I looked over to Sharon and Alex seated together. Alex had his gigantic right hand on Sharon's knee, and she had both of her hands over his. Sharon appeared to be in ecstasy; Alex's face, however, was like a stone—emotionless, white.

Joey and Sean went through two more rounds. Each was more ferocious than the previous one. Joey was deemed the winner, but it was close. The crowd gave a standing ovation.

The next fight matched Seth against Danny. The bell rang and they lunged toward each other like two wildcats on meth, but after a ten-second flurry of punches, Danny hit the floor like he'd been shot with a gun—his knees just buckled, and his body fell to a thud. Seth was as amazed as anyone. Danny was motionless. Junior gave him smelling salts. He rolled on his side. The fight was called.

Each bout was as feral as the last one. And then it was my turn. By this point, I thought—maybe this is what it means to be non-identified—I didn't care about whatever pain I had coming to me. Edgar and I touched gloves and began to punch the shit out of each other. The three rounds were a blur of the yelling crowd, hot lights, continual pummeling of each other, and endless sweat and pain. When it was over, it was deemed a draw. I felt like a world champion. The crowd roared. Edgar and I hugged, and we congratulated each other.

We all hit the showers and were proud and elated that it was over and that nobody had died. While we were getting dressed for the last time in that moldy, stinky locker room near the Brooklyn and Manhattan Bridges, Glen came in and said that we would be going to a restaurant on Mott Street in Chinatown. When we got to the restaurant our class was already there, including Sharon, seated at a head table with Fred. We had the place all to ourselves. Everyone stood as we entered, and they gave us an ovation. We all clapped too. It was said that it was important to clap for oneself in order to break "Identification."

We took our seats and as we quieted down Sharon spoke to us about how proud she was of the men and how well we had done. She said that this Line of Work was possible because of the power of School and the result of "Conscious Suffering." She said, "There is no pleasure unless there is suffering. Tonight was a display of sublime pleasure—the creation of sexual energy which we can use to create souls." Fred nodded solemnly.

Happy, Not Merry, Christmas

When we exited the Space at 7:00 a.m., lower Broadway was covered with ten inches of snow. A cabbie was gunning his engine, his tires spinning hopelessly. It was still coming down heavy. My classmate Barbara and I marveled at each snowflake dancing down to the earth from the white heavens—no two the same—forming a uniform silky cover over these hard sidewalks. School had spent the entire night and early morning dancing, feasting, celebrating during this most fecund, miraculous time—Christmas—where we celebrate the birth of a conscious man. As students—no two the same, coming from the heavens—we were also creating a cover, a protection over a dark and hard world. The 1992 Christmas "Class" was just letting out. It had been a miraculous night, further binding our community, our devotion to School, its teachers, and Sharon. On the empty pre-rush-hour subway back home, I was overcome by serenity and well-being. It's a rare feeling, a long-lost feeling. I wanted to spend the rest of my life in the Work—protected in the secrecy of School while going about my life as a New Yorker. I wanted, as Fred would say, to have my life blend or integrate with the Work. I would be helping to save civilization, to save the planet. Such was the affirming effect of this sublime Christmas Class.

Preparations for Christmas Class had begun in late October. "It's a class, not a party. It's for learning," Fred had explained. "It's also a gift from us to Sharon and must be prepared for with a great deal of consciousness and Aim. We must strive for perfection." Finally, he said, "It's also a time of year when there are so many negative influences: commercialization, identification with family obligations, associations with the past, and so on. This class will help you to remember yourselves and celebrate the true meanings of Christmas." Unlike the past years in School where we had an informal cocktail party for a few hours, Fred said we were now ready to have a "Conscious Party." It was to be a black-tie affair that would be held in the Space. And with this, we started our work. We were broken up into committees and we met for several hours after every class, into the early morning, sometimes until 4:00 a.m. (and also for full days on the weekends) to prepare: we designed, constructed, and installed elaborate decorations; we cooked, and taste-tested food; we rehearsed scenes from plays; we rehearsed dance pieces; we worked on set lists for DJ'd music; we formed a choir to sing Christmas songs; and we discussed our internal Aims, to make the Work practical. We spent hundreds of hours getting it ready.

This preparation time meant time away from families, friends, and other holiday obligations; this created conflict for many of us, especially those who celebrated Christmas. Those who had families out of town were told not to go away until at least Christmas Eve day (we usually held the class the week before Christmas). Fred said that the less time spent with family the better because the holiday had too many "associations and identifications." When people said they were going home to visit their families for the holidays, he immediately corrected them, saying, "New York is your home." He spent hours during class helping people to figure out ways to condense or cancel out-of-town trips. People with spouses and children outside School had to carefully plan how to be out of the house for so many hours. Almost all married students reported during the holidays that their spouses assumed they were having affairs (some were). Fred counseled students that their spouses were being unreasonable and hinted that these marriages were unstable or doomed (many did fail). Although my family did not celebrate Christmas, I usually saw my mother and Matthew at some point in December for a Hanukkah dinner, but it had to be planned for a non-School night.

Finally, the night arrived. Every detail was perfect. The walls were covered with tapestries and oversized reproductions of famous Renaissance paintings depicting the life of Christ. The Space's eighteen-foot-high tin ceilings were covered with dozens of rows of white Christmas lights. On the back wall hung a reproduction of Chartres's stained-glass windows. In the center of the room was a decorative fountain. Our hand-hewn mahogany bar was stocked with every top-shelf liquor, including expensive bottles of wine and port. A huge U-shaped table filled the room, enough to seat sixty of us,[15] covered with candles, pine branches, papier-mâché statuettes of figures of the Holy Family and three Kings, and place settings. The head table—for the six teachers from New York and six from Boston—was festooned somewhat more elaborately and with place settings of fine china, silverware, and a handmade tablecloth. Sharon's setting, in the center, had a miniature crèche scene; her seat was a throne. The food was kept in chafing dishes warmed by Sterno in the back room, but we could smell the five-course feast—curries, biryani, poori, paratha, soups, papadum, aloo matar, chana masala, paneer tikka masala—some of which would be passed around during cocktail hour as hors d'oeuvres. Bach's Christmas Oratorio played on the sound system. A large Christmas tree was in the corner. Most every teacher in School—Sharon, Fred, Robert—was Jewish.

At 8:00 p.m., Sharon appeared to find us assembled in formal wear singing a rousing version of "Hark! The Herald Angels Sing." She beamed in her floor-length, low-cut black dress, and diamonds. Alex was not with her, but Joshua attended as her escort. We had cocktails, mingled, and then the room was set up for "presentations." Students performed scenes from Shakespeare and Chekov, songs, poems, comedy sketches, choral pieces, and belly dancing. I played bass, accompanying someone singing Sandy Denny's "Who Knows Where the Time Goes?" Peterson sang a slightly out-of-tune but

---

15 Each class in New York and Boston held their own Christmas Class but on different nights with different decorations, music, performances, and so Sharon and the other teachers attended several different parties in the week leading up to Christmas Day.

soulful version of Elton John's "Love Song." Sharon was ecstatic, like she was during the boxing matches. Fred stood behind her, massaging her shoulders, also looking blissful. At a certain point, she and the other teachers went back into the teachers' office, and the room was readied for dinner, whereafter she made another grand entrance, to the recording of Bach's *Cello Suites* performed by Pablo Casals. We were seated according to a seating chart, determined by Sharon— her favorite, most devoted students, sat closest to her, in descending order. If you were seated in the back, you were on the outs, literally. I was placed right next to the teacher's table. We stood and held hands while grace was read by Fred—Matthew 7:1-5:

> Judge not, that ye be not judged.
>
> For with what judgment ye judge, ye shall be judged: and with what measure ye mete, it shall be measured to you again.
>
> And why beholdest thou the mote that is in thy brother's eye, but considerest not the beam that is in thine own eye?
>
> Or how wilt thou say to thy brother, Let me pull out the mote out of thine eye; and, behold, a beam is in thine own eye?
>
> Thou hypocrite, first cast out the beam out of thine own eye; and then shalt thou see clearly to cast out the mote out of thy brother's eye.

Sharon moaned, and then the teachers moaned, and so did the class. Sharon said "Amen." Then Sharon spoke: "Thank you. Happy Christmas. You have made a beautiful night. You should all be proud of yourselves. We are building a real school. Anything you can imagine, you can create. Christmas is a time for expanding relationships. This does not mean buying presents for your family. It means opening your hearts to everyone. Christ says: 'Love your enemies,' but you can't love enemies if you don't even love your Essence friends. In order to be a good Christian, one must 'be.'" Sharon continued in this vein for another hour and a half. The room was poorly ventilated, hot, lit only by candles and Christmas lights, and smelled vaguely of curry. As Sharon spoke, some students nodded off—it was now 1:15 a.m. Finally, Sharon looked at Fred and said, "Shall we eat?" Fred gave a signal and the students who were assigned to be waiters for the night brought in dinner and joined us at the tables. The food was stone cold. Sharon screamed, "This food is frozen. What kind of Christmas gift is this? Are you trying to kill me?" She launched into a blistering attack on the class for our "weak beings" and "hearts as cold as the chicken." After forty-five minutes of railing, she stood and left with the teachers trailing. The tables were cleared and moved. The music changed to rock and roll. We danced until 6:00 a.m. We cleaned up the Space. We left at 7:00 a.m. It was snowing.

Sharon Gans and Robert Klein at a Christmas Class. Circa 1996. Used with permission.

Fred Mindel. Circa 1996. Used with permission.

The Ranch That
Consciousness Built

The back porch ran the length of the chalet, which had a cupola that was sheathed with cedar thatch shingles. The lawn in the half-acre backyard was always cut, but Montana grass is thick and unruly. In the center of the yard stood a fountain with a bronze sculpture of a nude woman pouring water from a pitcher she cradled like a child. Pine trees four stories high surrounded the yard creating a protective, hidden sanctuary beneath the big Montana sky. Here Sharon's most favored students gathered for more than a week every summer. I spent weeks meeting on that porch almost every summer from 1993 through 2012. I remember it all—the bliss, clarity, inspiration, love, anger, panic, enlightenment, tears, shame, violence, and madness.

School's wonders never ended until the end. But until the end, Sharon let on in dribs and drabs what it was all about. Everyone loved the suspense. It was like an immersive mystery. It kept us on our toes. So, in June 1993, a secret invitation was offered to a select group of about twenty students from our class, including Seth, Sara, Raymond, Sam, Jeff, Brian, George, Marion, Harvey, Kim, Patrice, Peter, and me. Fred said, "Sharon is inviting you to work closely with her for several days. It's the greatest honor that could be granted by Sharon. It's called Retreat and it's the sun of the year which all else revolves around." He said we would be traveling by plane to get there and that our destination was isolated, that we wouldn't be told where we were going until we got there, and we wouldn't be able to be in touch with anyone for those ten days. We were to pack dress clothes and work clothes we could throw away. He said to pack boots and sneakers. It was Sharon's acknowledgment of our place in the hierarchy of School. Part of the reason we were selected was because Sharon believed we had great "possibilities" and were on the cusp of elevating to a new level. He said Retreat is a "pressure cooker" and we should expect to work hard—inwardly and outwardly. The cost was $1,200 (cash, in advance) plus the cost of round-trip air travel. Fred said to bring some extra spending money. Those of us who had children under thirteen were invited to bring them along. Fred warned us not to tell any other students about our new secret.

It was my fourth anniversary in School—July 1993—and we met at JFK at the crack of dawn. Jimmy, a new teacher, was waiting there for us at curbside. He had just started teaching about six months before, having attended the recently held bowling-class-outside-of-class. He was younger than the other teachers—about my age—and he was informal, cerebral, and gentle. Jimmy handed us our tickets but told us not to look at the destination or the gate number so we could receive a "Conscious Shock." He walked us to the gate and we all deliberately avoided looking at the destination posted at the gate. On the flight we saw Sharon in first class, and she waved hello to us as we walked back to economy.[16] We connected in Salt Lake City, and were led to another gate by Fred, who met us in the airport at Salt Lake. We only learned where we were headed when the captain announced that we were on the connecting flight to Kalispell, a place I'd never heard of; I didn't even know what state we were headed to. The flight was about an hour, and we could see we were landing in a place surrounded by snowcapped mountains. We deplaned and met at the baggage claim. When we got into the terminal, I discovered we were in northwestern Montana, near the entrance to Glacier National Park.

After our bags came, right near the carousel, Fred gathered us in a circle and we huddled around Sharon. She was radiating, "Welcome

---

16 I learned later that a portion of the $1,200 we each paid to attend Retreat went to the cost of buying Sharon's first-class round-trip tickets.

to Montana!" We got into two vans and drove off, Sharon in a separate car with Fred. I'd never even been in the Rockies.

We drove through downtown Kalispell on the way to Sharon's remote ranch. The town looked just like the set of a western movie. L. Ron Hubbard had lived there as a child.

The ranch was in the town of Condon, Montana, population three hundred, about sixty-four miles south of Kalispell. It sat between the Swan Mountain Range on the east and the Mission Mountains on the west, adjacent to the Bob Marshall Wilderness Area, known as "the Bob" by the locals. Over a million acres and stretching sixty miles along the continental divide, the Bob is said to have the largest population of grizzly bears in the contiguous United States. It's also home to moose, elk, black bears, mountain goats, bighorn sheep, coyotes, wolverines, mountain lions, lynx, and wolf. Bald eagles and ospreys can be spotted and heard among the dense old-growth forests, which have Douglas fir, larch, and spruce.

We sat in silence in the van. We were tired from the excitement and travel and were taking in the majesty of the place. It looked like pictures I'd seen of the Swiss Alps. Our driver, Norman—an older student from Boston whom I'd never met—barely spoke. There was something about him that was familiar. Although a stranger, we spoke the same Work language and lived by the same School-code. He wore suspenders. We were comrades in the Work and bound by the invisible world. Whenever we met someone else in School for the first time, it was like we were meeting a distant cousin who sounded and looked like us.

We slowed as we entered Condon, which had a post office, a motel, and a combination Sinclair gas station and general store. About a mile outside town, Norman turned left onto a dirt road. We were silent. It was bone dry and the van kicked up dust, practically whiting out the windows. But we could make out that we were headed into the deep wilderness. After two miles we reached the end of the road and passed through gates which said PRIVATE. The road threaded through a forest, four stories high. Finally, we came upon a single-story log cabin in the woods, the size of a tennis court. Just beyond it, we came into our destination: The Falls Creek Ranch.

We got out of our van and waited for the van following us to pull up and let out its passengers. A hundred yards away was a several-acre lake, and beyond that there were trees stretching out for miles, headed up the western mountain range of the Bob. Above the tree lines were bare mountain rock peaks and then the snowcaps. In summer. We were speechless. Sharon walked over to us, escorted by Fred. She welcomed us to her ranch. We all thanked her for inviting us. Sharon explained that the ranch had been built entirely by her students, under the influence and edicts of the Work. She'd designed it.

This was a big secret to be let in on. Still, every School revelation raised more questions for me. Who paid for this? Who built it? Why did Sharon have a place in Montana? Did she have a family beyond her absent husband, Alex? How often did people come here? I said to Sharon, "This place is majestic," to which she responded, "Well, now it's all just for you."

Sharon went on: "You will all be making daily internal Aims to work on yourself and making external Aims to complete certain projects. The point is not to work on projects—the point is to work on yourselves, with Aim. This ranch is about consciousness. Can you feel it here?" The men would work on construction projects and the women would work in the kitchen, preparing the three meals a day and helping with the three young children who had come with their parents. Every afternoon we were to meet on the porch behind Sharon's home to read and discuss one of Dr. Nicol's *Psychological Commentaries on the Teaching of Gurdjieff and Ouspensky*.[17] At each meeting, we'd make new Aims for the following day. She told us to take notes, because in the spring we'd write a paper for her about our lives. (Retreats were the only occasions we were allowed to take notes.)

Sharon gave us a tour. On the north side of the lake there were four log cabins known as Cabin 4, Cabin 5, Cabin 6, and Cabin 7.

---

17 Maurice Nicol, an acolyte of Ouspensky and Gurdjieff, was a Scottish psychiatrist who wrote the five-volume *Psychological Commentaries on the Teaching of Gurdjieff and Ouspensky*, which contains hundreds of lectures he gave to study groups.

Although they were of slightly varied sizes and designs, they each had the same floor plan: a deck, a central room with a kitchen, several beds on the first floor and then a loft with a few more beds. They each had wood stoves. The bathrooms had tiny cedar shower stalls whose curtains hung from a rod made of a tree branch. The structures were solid and well crafted. Although Spartan, they were clean and comfortable. They all looked out at the lake. On the south side of the lake were Cabin 1, Cabin 2, and Cabin 3. Cabin 1 was a larger structure that had two different buildings connected by a breezeway. It had a floor-to-ceiling window overlooking the lake. It was unfathomable how just students of the Work could have built this. But we knew Sharon would not entertain questions and nobody dared to ask.[18]

On the western side of the lake were two large log structures: the Guest House and the Main House. The Main House, a chalet, was Sharon's house. It was built on a hill towering over the property and had a grand deck on the east which faced the lake and the spectacular views of the Bob. From that grand deck, you could make out the namesake of the ranch, a dozen miles away up in the mountains: the Falls Creek waterfalls, which eventually emptied into the ranch's lake. At the foot of the Main House was a grassy hill bordered by Falls Creek, which snaked around the house like a deep moat, separating her home from the rest of the property. Over the creek there was a small, covered bridge. Another important feature of the property were the tiny islands in the center of the lake. One island was attached to a large wooden bridge, in the shape of a rainbow—the "Rainbow Bridge"—and the other island was attached by the "Chinese Bridge."

The Guest House contained two spacious rooms: the kitchen and the dining room. It also had a basement with a walk-in refrigerator, laundry machines, a darkroom, and bathrooms. In addition to two long tables, the dining room had old couches and a large window

---

18 I recently learned that the seven cabins were substantially built by just four students who spent about eight months in Montana working sixteen-hour days. They not only worked without pay, but they were paying tuition at the time. The conditions were brutal and in the dead of winter. They worked under impossible deadlines set by Alex and Sharon. If they were built today, it's estimated it would have cost $3 million to build them.

overlooking the lake, the Rainbow Bridge, and the Bob. There were several large hunting trophies on the wall: two elk, two deer, and a moose. The dining room had a heavy oak door with an elk's antler as the handle. This room functioned as the living room and dining room for Retreat.

We learned that the first structure we'd seen as we drove onto the property contained a large heated indoor swimming pool, with the tile design of a parrot, plus a sauna and a bathroom. Sharon said it was her favorite place on the ranch and was her "temple." One of us was assigned to check the pool temperature three times a day to ensure it was exactly at eighty-four degrees. The building was off-limits unless permission was sought and granted directly by Sharon. She skinny-dipped there every afternoon.

This over-the-top creature comfort—an ornate heated indoor swimming pool built deep in the middle of nowhere solely for skinny-dipping—was hard to reconcile with the strictly internal premises of the Work. I knew the Work was not for the ascetic, but this was luxury on a different level. I wondered whether anyone else noticed the contradiction. They did. But nobody voiced it. Silence. Discordance. Tucked away.

The ranch also had horse stables, and one of us was assigned to care for the horses. The ranch had caretakers—Mary and Frank—who lived in town and were not privy to School; they were told we were part of Sharon's acting troupe from New York.

Finally, Sharon led us down a road to a point about two hundred yards to the north of the Pool House. Here was a partially dug foundation for a future large structure. Beyond it was a basketball court (a large chessboard painted on the court) and beyond that a clay tennis court. Near the new structure, there were dozens of enormous logs: they were about four feet in diameter and twenty feet long, cut from trees that were hundreds of years old. Sharon said that this structure was going to be a theater, her dream. She called it "Karnak," but told us that only she was allowed to say its name. She said it was the final project for the ranch and that we were going to help construct it.

Falls Creek Ranch. Courtesy of Kevin Wetherell.

Sharon's indoor pool. Courtesy of Kevin Wetherell.

Karnak. Courtesy of Kevin Wetherell.

Until the moment we arrived at Kalispell, all we knew about Sharon was her first name and her husband. She never divulged any personal details about herself. I didn't know where she lived, what she did for a living (except that she was once an actress), or whether she even had children. The mystery and intrigue made me guess and want to know more. On the other hand, we had a bargain in School—we were bound by ideas and inner qualities, not by the externals. So, in a sense this other stuff—people's personal lives—was irrelevant. When we came to the ranch, it was the most information about Sharon that she had shared. There were many questions the ranch raised, but I was on overload already.

Sharon's obvious wealth did not give me any pause in terms of my faith in her and the Work. I knew Sharon must have had a large income from School: I knew how to multiply the number of people in School by the monthly tuition, and I knew it was all in cash.[19] But this didn't really matter to me. The fees I paid were fair, and I didn't care how Sharon spent it. After all, she was generously allowing us to come to her ranch and had given me so much.

I didn't think there was anything hypocritical about claiming to be a highly conscious person interested in evolution and to also have a heated indoor pool in Montana with a tile parrot. I kind of liked it. I didn't want to be ashamed of my own materialism. I didn't want to be St. Francis. It was a little refreshing to see materialism and consciousness were not mutually exclusive. This also confirmed my belief that the Work ideas—including Aim—would help me attain wealth.

---

19   In addition to monthly tuition, which ranged anywhere from $300 to $500 depending upon when the student joined, there were other fees. We paid $100 annually to Sharon's "retirement fund." We paid $10 weekly toward an orphanage fund. We paid a $50 monthly "maintenance fee" which went towards rent, utilities, and other monthly expenses of the Space. For people who went on Retreat, in addition to the $1,200 fee to attend and round-trip airfare, we paid over $1,000 annually for the ranch's property taxes and upkeep. All Christmas parties and the birthday parties were paid entirely by the students: usually $300 per year. Plus, we paid another $200 annually for Sharon's Christmas gift. Acting classes cost a few hundred dollars per month; we had to pay for boxing. We contributed toward construction projects. These fees were in addition to the value of free labor given to Sharon.

After Sharon's tour, we were assigned cabins. I shared one with Sam and Raymond. We made fires in the woodstoves—in July. We walked over to the Guest House at around 10:00 p.m., the air filled with the smell of wood smoke, and it was still light. We had a spaghetti dinner. It was festive but Sharon did not attend. We finished up at about 3:00 a.m. My cabinmates left before me, so I walked back to the cabin alone, about three hundred yards, without a flashlight. It was moonless, pitch black, and the Milky Way filled the heavens. As I approached the cabin deck, I heard what was either coyotes or wolves howling, way in the distance, spooky as hell. I ran into the fucking cabin and locked the door, my cabinmates cracking up.

It was 5:30 a.m., forty-six degrees, and ten guys from New York City with soft hands walked through the dewy Montana grass to start the project. Bundled up in work clothes and on an hour of sleep, we came upon a black bear and her cubs crossing our path about twenty-five yards ahead. They hustled off when they heard us. When we got to Karnak there was an elk who we also spooked. Crows and other birds signaled our arrival. Fresh mountain air. We had been instructed to strip the gigantic logs for Sharon's theater in the woods. Seth noted that there were going to be far more wild animals there than paying theatergoers.

Fred arrived late, apparently having overslept. We gathered up the tools: hand axes, debarking tools, and double-handed curved draw shaving tools, foreign objects to us all. We had no idea what we were doing. But the job was intuitive. We spent ten minutes gathered in a huddle, one by one stating individual internal Aims. "To practice non-identification with the body." "To remember myself." "To observe internal complaints." Mine was "to be in 'True Personality,' not 'False Personality.'" Fred liked mine because one of the images of False Personality was that it was a like mold which grew on the bark of trees—bark was considered True Personality that protected the Essence or the wood under the bark.

These enormous logs were recently felled and wet, making the bark difficult to remove. The outer bark came off easily, but then there were thin layers of skin that we were told needed to be scraped off. The logs changed colors and it was hard to tell exactly what was skin and what was wood. Fred said it was important not to strip off any of the wood. It was exhausting and tedious. The high altitude made it harder to breathe. The Montana mosquitoes are big, loud, and impervious to anything but Ben's 100 DEET, which none of us had packed. Within minutes I realized what we were doing was nuts and wondered why Sharon didn't just hire someone to do this. Finally, we went to breakfast at the Guest House at 9:00 a.m.

The women had prepared the Hungry Man's Breakfast, straight off the menu from every diner in Manhattan: pancakes covered with two over-easy eggs, a side of bacon and sausage, hash browns, home-made biscuits with gravy, coffee, orange juice. Nothing had ever tasted better. It was casual and fun in the homey dining room. Like summer camp, but with much better food. Fred held an organizational meet-ing that included the fire safety plan and how to behave when seeing wild animals. After breakfast, we worked for another couple of hours until the afternoon meeting was to be held.

At 12:45 p.m., we dropped what we were doing and walked up the hill to Sharon's back porch, silently. By now it was a dry seventy degrees, not a cloud in the sky. Red-tailed hawks soared overhead. It was the first time I saw Sharon's half-acre backyard. It was planted with gardens and, except for the tall conifers, it reminded me of my childhood backyard in Levittown—although one of the trees looked as if it functioned as a back scratcher for grizzlies. We set up the stackable white plastic chairs in a semicircle under the cupola, with Sharon's black mesh outdoor recliner on one end. We sat silently reading commentaries, and at 1:10 p.m., Sharon appeared at the far end of the porch, walked the twenty feet to us and smiled—we stood and welcomed her. Fred helped her into her seat. She sprayed on Ben's 100 DEET. She was wearing sunglasses and a black dress, and had on her white Converse sneakers. "Let's begin," she said, "who has a commentary for us today?" Several of us read out titles from *Psychological Commentaries on the Teaching of Gurdjieff and Ouspensky*, until Sharon settled on one picked by Sasha, who was a teacher from

Boston. It was entitled "On the Selection of Thoughts." Sharon nodded, and Sasha read:

> It is very important to select your thoughts—that is, the lines
> of thought that you will think along. People complain that they
> cannot think. The reason why is that they do not start from a
> thought or an idea. In order to think you must have a definite
> thought or idea. But these thoughts or ideas come to us as a kind
> of inflow, and we can only select which to go with and which not
> to go with. For example, if you have a thought or an idea enter-
> ing your mind, say, the thought that no one likes you, it is just as
> well not to think this. So you must understand that you may have
> a thought but not think it, just as you may have a sword in your
> hand and not use it. . . . You are not responsible for your thoughts
> unless you think them. And if you can see that the thought is
> false, you certainly will not think it—that is, follow it out to the
> conclusion to which it leads. When you are negative you receive
> nothing but false thoughts—in short, evil thoughts. But although
> it is your fault possibly that you are negative, it is not your fault
> that these thoughts come to you, because they belong to that
> realm of the mind which is called Hell and from which we have
> to free ourselves if we are given the possibility of doing so.

Sharon sighed loudly, exclaiming, "This is brilliant and is perfect for
today. Retreat is magic because this is exactly what we needed to
hear today." Sasha seconded this, saying she picked it because it is so
"forgiving." We nodded in agreement.

After a few people spoke, I confessed that I had negative thoughts
while stripping the logs. I also admitted that I was having the thought
that Sharon should hire someone from Kalispell to strip the logs. Sharon broke into hearty laughter and everyone else joined. Smiling, but
with those eyes fixed on me like the red dot from a Glock, she said,
"Working hard is a privilege, it's for you, to help you grow internally.
I could easily hire someone to do this work, but what good would
that do you? School is an artificial cosmos." I knew this. And then
she continued, "It's not our fault if negative thoughts come into our

head, but it is our fault if we choose to think them. We have a choice to select other thoughts and not think those thoughts. These negative thoughts are just like little birds in your head—just let them come in one ear and out the other."

I wondered whether I could actually select thoughts that were positive. It seemed like a game changer. The high altitude, hard work, and little sleep made me loopy, drunk. This spectacular, isolated setting; this intimate group of Sharon's twenty closest, best students. I was here. It all combined to make this moment overwhelmingly powerful, magnifying every remark, gesture, statement, and look Sharon gave.

At about 3:00 p.m., Sharon stopped the discussion and asked us to formulate internal Aims for the next twenty-four hours. The Aims had to correlate to the commentary and to individual instructions given to us. We read them out loud one at a time. Sharon would either signal approval or ask for it to be rewritten. Before we were dismissed at about 3:30 p.m., she asked us to spend fifteen minutes "mentating" alone in a quiet spot on the ranch and then fifteen minutes of "sitting." When someone asked for instructions, she explained that "mentating is mentating and sitting is sitting." Fred laughed and so did Sharon.[20]

Lunch was served at about 4:00 p.m. It was festive, hectic, and loud. The children were there, and were happy to be reunited with their parents, because during the day they were tended to by female students who acted as camp counselors. Sharon attended, sitting at the head of her table flanked by Fred and Robert. We chatted among ourselves; it was informal. At about 5:00 p.m. Sharon headed back to her house and there was an hour of "family time" where we could rest. We got back to work at 6:00 p.m. until 8:30 p.m., when we quit for the day, showered, and met back at the Guest House for dinner. The women wore dresses and the men were in business-casual clothes. When Sharon entered, we stood, and when she got to her seat

---

20 According to Anthony Storr, English psychiatrist and author of several books including his 1996 *Feet of Clay; Saints, Sinners, and Madmen: A Study of Gurus* (which includes Gurdjieff as a subject of study), "*chronic schizophrenics often invent words which carry a special meaning for them but which others find hard to understand.*"

at the head table, we joined hands and waited for her to select someone to say grace, an honor bestowed upon someone for exceptional
work that day. Then we dined on grilled steak, corn on the cob, and
red wine. We spent hours eating, talking, laughing, sometimes someone would play guitar or sing or play piano. At around 11:00 p.m.,
Sharon quieted the room for the evening meeting, the bookend to
the afternoon commentary meeting.

Each of us spoke, one at a time, for twenty to thirty minutes, stating our Aims out loud, and reflecting on our inner experiences of the
day. Sharon reserved high praise for our work during this meeting,
encouraging and supporting our inner work to practice the ideas of
the commentary and to apply the help she gave. But I noticed the
meeting got competitive: We tried to outdo each other in having the
bigger breakthrough, epiphany, transformation, or deeper moment of
Self-Remembering. We spoke in lofty and poetic ways, feeling safe to
express our deepest feelings, memories, and wishes.

At some point during this meeting, I stopped, took in the
room: the enormous animal trophies, the emotional faces of my
friends, the glow of the candles, the smell of Montana pines, and
the voices of each speaker, as if it was frozen in time. I imagined
an impartial observer. What would they think of this? Could they
understand it?

Sharon loved these meetings and seemed to be fed by our work
and experiences and she reminded us of our privilege to be working
together. The meeting ended around 2:00 a.m. It took an hour to
clean up. Wake-up was at 5:00 a.m.

The next morning work on the logs continued despite a serious
storm that caused some flooding and loss of power in several cabins.
We worked in ponchos, still soaked, in pain from pummeling Montana rain and mosquitoes. Montana mud is clay, impossible to move
in and remove from drenched work boots. Fred said to us, "These are
perfect conditions for you to transform negative thoughts. After all,
these are minor temporary discomforts." But by the fourth day of this
I was spent. I couldn't "work on myself" and be positive. I was cranky,
sore, blistered, and angry. Very cranky. I just couldn't seem to "select"
positive thoughts.

During the commentary meeting behind Sharon's house that day, Sam (the tall playwright from the South) started to do Second Line of Work: he told Sharon that I had been unpleasant and cranky all day and he didn't like it. To engage in Second Line of Work, one needs not to be judgmental, but humble and modest. What you say to another you need to say to yourself. Sam was very good at Second Line of Work and enjoyed doing it. I, however, never liked being on the other end of his work. Sam said, "Spencer, I see something in you that I see in myself which I have been trying to root out for years. You were very irritable and unpleasant this morning." Sharon jumped in, "Sam, this is good work, and brave of you to say. This will help your friend." I jumped in to say that I was tired, had very dark thoughts, and I couldn't select any other thoughts Raymond also liked to do Second Line of Work and said that "Spencer Schneider is a bear." Using my full name was a reference to my False Personality and not me—my real self is in Essence and True Personality. Sharon saw my distress and jumped back in, "Nobody is insulting you, Spencer—they were ridiculing your False Personality, which only deserves to be ridiculed. Try to take in what is being said. This is all for learning."

I wasn't feeling the love. I was exhausted, miserable during the next work period. I was distant. I also concluded that I was weak since nobody else was complaining about the fatigue and hard work and mosquitoes. At the dinner meeting, I told Sharon that I had not been a great athlete growing up and that the work on the logs was bringing up those memories and attendant emotions. After speaking for a few minutes, Sharon said to me, "No, Spencer, you are a very strong and healthy man, and you can do anything. I saw you in the boxing ring and how brave you were. I also peeked at the men working on the logs. You are as strong and as hard a worker as anyone. You don't see yourself this way. You see yourself as weak." And then she said this: "You were babied by your mother and internalized her fears." This was not my impression of my mother—she never discouraged me from physical activities. I was put to work every weekend by my parents, and I had part-time jobs since I was thirteen—my mother never babied me.

But when Sharon made these kinds of remarks, in the secluded woods of Montana, surrounded by my friends, after four intense days of labor, little sleep, and the desire to be working on myself and get her approval—and because nobody dared to disagree with her—it was impossible not to believe what she was saying. When Sharon gave help to other students, she would almost always say something that was persuasive. She would have the floor and make a case about some quality about that person, and it would stick. There was usually an ounce of truth about that quality, and she would just build off that. Before you knew it, she was speaking the obvious total truth and it seemed like a keen observation. For instance, Mark was below average height. Sharon maintained that he was insecure about it, and this colored everything he did, and led to many other insecurities of his—about women, about his work as a scientist, and how he related to other people, which she claimed was passive-aggressive. Aside from being shorter, I hadn't noticed Mark as having any of those qualities; but when Sharon said it, everyone was persuaded—even Mark. And if you didn't believe it then you eventually would.

On one of the last nights of Retreat, Sharon said that the men should go skinny-dipping in her pool. We jumped in and did cannon balls off the diving board. Afterward, Robert asked us to join him in the sauna, a cramped little room that fit four comfortably. We were nine sitting shoulder to shoulder, nude. We were tired so nobody cared. But Robert seemed to be having the most fun. He started to sing some of those western-themed campfire songs. I'd never seen him so happy and relaxed. But I wasn't comfortable.

On the last night of Retreat, Sharon invited us to have dinner in her home. Unlike the Spartan but comfortable accommodations on the rest of the ranch, Sharon's home had fine furniture, art, rugs, and fixtures, including a Tiffany lamp. Hanging over the fireplace was an enormous portrait of Anton Chekhov, one of her heroes, painted by Simon. After the meeting we stated our "Mantras," which consisted of an accumulation of our daily Aims along with three "reasons" for making these Aims. When we got back to New York we were to interrupt our days at five designated times, no matter what we were doing, find a private place, and say our Mantras out loud to ourselves.

(Sharon instructed me and one of the other lawyers that if we were in front of a judge at a designated time, we should postpone saying our Mantra until after the session ended; this was also granted to another student who was an emergency room doctor.)

We returned to Manhattan from Retreat exhausted and pushed to the limit—but we were a closer-knit group within a group. It had been a trial by fire, people had revealed themselves, and the bond was strengthened.

Sharon stayed in Montana—she still had two more Retreats with the other classes that lasted into August. She returned to New York in mid-October.

Sharon Nights, Part II

B ack in New York, Sean was having problems with his new
marriage and stood up for help. Married for two weeks, his
wife was insisting on knowing his whereabouts on Tuesday and
Thursday nights. Sean had been clinging steadfast to Fred's instruction to "be firm" and to say "it's none of your business" when she
asked where he was going in the evening. On Sharon's first night
back Sean asked Sharon for help, "Sharon, my wife is threatening to
leave me." Sharon spoke, "Sean if you don't stand firm on this, your
marriage will be all wrong. It will fail. Women try to exercise power
in a relationship. It's our nature. And I understand that. But the man
leads, just like in dancing. That's the way of the universe. Women
love to be led. If you stand firm and lead like a man, she will get in
line and let you live your life. What you do in your personal life is
none of her fucking business." Sean worked as a lawyer for one of
the most prestigious law firms in New York. He was one of the most
obedient and willing people in School, very inspirational to people
like me who sometimes questioned or even challenged help. Sean
did in fact "stand firm" with his wife and the next day she sought
(and later obtained) an annulment. When Sharon came back to class
the following week, she said to Sean, "This was meant to be. This
woman was a rotten bitch, all mixed up. She did you a favor. Sean,
there are other women who would be dying to be with you." Sean

was bereft, but he took it with a stiff upper lip. He had been so happy to get married.[21]

For a few years, Marcie and her husband had been trying to have a child. She had had one miscarriage and was now having difficulty getting pregnant. They had just seen a fertility expert who suggested artificial insemination, in vitro fertilization, or the possibility of a surrogate mother. But Sharon had previously told Marcie that she should adopt a child. Sharon had told the class several times that any child born by any of those methods was akin to a "Frankenstein" who would "lack a soul." Marcie came into class that night to tell Sharon about her recent visit to a fertility expert. Sharon cut her off, shouting, "You are a piece of shit, and you would make a miserable mother. How dare you ignore my help." Hazel, in a show of loyalty to Sharon, stood up and called Marcie a "fucking liar." Marcie then did something I'd never seen anyone do up until this time: She stood up and said, "Fuck you Sharon," and started to walk out. Sharon shrieked, "You little cunt. If you leave, you will be killing all your possibilities." But Marcie didn't say a word, grabbed her coat, and ran out. A few people started to chase after her, but Sharon shouted, "No let her go, she will be back. I'll call her tomorrow." But we did not hear from Marcie, and she was missed terribly.

A few weeks later we had the annual Christmas Class. Sharon invited several people from the Boston group to attend. They were strangers but were like family, comrades in the Work. I noticed that one of our classmates, a woman named Maria, danced several times with a Boston student named Moshe. By the end of the evening,

---

21 This happened to Norm, as well, except that his marriage lasted less than two weeks. Marriage after marriage between students and nonstudents ended over this issue. This also happened with School marriages when one spouse left and the other stayed. Sharon and Fred would often explain to the remaining spouse that the spouse who had left would hurt their possibilities in School. Occasionally the remaining spouse would also leave School, but more often they would stay in School and just divorce the spouse who left. This was one reason why spouses in School marriages did not leave School if they valued their marriage. This happened to me.

they were kissing passionately. I had heard that Sharon had brought the Boston group so that Moshe could meet Maria. After that night, we never saw Maria again. She moved to Boston the following week, got married to Moshe in a matter of weeks, and they started a family.

Arthur was a physics professor, had a crew cut, and rarely smiled. He was the nerdiest guy in School, but a sweet man. I liked him, we all did. The few times he spoke in class, it was about his shyness and insecurities with women. One night, Sharon asked Arthur to take a seat in front that faced the room. She had him shut his eyes. Then she asked six women (some of them married) to come up to Arthur and massage him. One for each limb, one for his neck and shoulders and one for his chest. Sharon, speaking in quiet tones, coached them: where to massage, the pressure, the direction. The lights in the room were dimmed. This went on for thirty minutes. Arthur was humiliated, but it seemed that Sharon was aroused. The rest of us were cringing, because we knew that if Sharon had asked the women to take Arthur in the back room and continue the experiment nude and "let it go from there," every one of them would have complied. But Arthur had reached his breaking point and was gone from School in a few weeks.

Another student, Elsa, had once been a fashion model. Sharon would occasionally make snide remarks about her looks, calling her superficial. She once told me privately that Elsa was a "walking vagina" with no soul. But one night Elsa spoke about her unhappy marriage. She had resisted Sharon's instructions to divorce her husband (who was not in School) and now she talked about her loneliness. Sharon took a new tack. "Elsa," Sharon intoned, "You need to get laid. Why don't you screw Donald?" Donald, mind you, was dating Norma, a wealthy widow who was in this class but not in attendance that night. Donald jumped to his feet so quickly that he practically fell forward. "Donald, you and Elsa should go to an all-night drugstore and purchase some condoms and body oils and lotions and make love all night long. Get a nice hotel room." Donald and Elsa looked at each other from across the room and smiled nervously. Class ended and they left together.[22] At the next class Sharon attended, Elsa stood to thank Sharon for her "beautiful" night with Donald. Sharon told her to "keep quiet and sit down."

Later that night, Sharon wished Fred a happy birthday. We all sang. She remarked that she and Fred were friends for a long time. Then she smiled and said in a half-joking manner, "Fred and I are friends that fuck." We all laughed, assuming this was just an off-color joke, but it was Fred who turned colors.

Two weeks later, however, Fred was gone.

We had arrived at Retreat just the day before. It was our second year in Montana. "I had to send Fred away from School—he stopped working on himself," Sharon said as she walked into the Guest House at lunch time. "He is now on a plane headed back to New York."

Sharon explained, "This is for his own good. He's now in the spiritual wilderness, and will have to fend for himself. It's wrong for him and the Work for him to be in School." She continued, "This is a great shock for you." Fred had been our main teacher from Day One and had taught practically every class for the past several years. Aside from Robert who seemed to be Sharon's right-hand man, Fred was her number two. There was no indication or warning sign. Just that morning he had been out with us working on another project, repairing the perimeter fence for her 125-acre property. Sharon warned us not to make any contact with him. She said that if we contacted him, it would "kill his possibilities" of returning to School.

---

22 This was the first time I heard Sharon give this kind of "help." I am told, however, that on Retreat some years before I came to School something similar happened. During a meeting, Sharon told one of her students—a shy young woman—that she too "needed to get laid." An older student was selected and the two of them immediately left to go to a cabin where they had sex. Sharon also privately encouraged hookups. On at least two occasions, she told me to sleep with certain women she thought I should like, but I chose not to. I did however have a few trysts with three other women (all in the acting class) without Sharon's advance knowledge, but I later told her about it.

And it would be a serious "leak" and hurt our own connections with School.

This year both Fred and our new teacher Jimmy had come out with us to Retreat, and Jimmy was in the room when Sharon made this announcement. Sharon explained that she had just learned that the logs had not been properly stripped the previous year and this was Fred's fault because he had been leading us. Some of the men agreed that Fred didn't seem to have a handle on how to strip the logs, but we were still surprised and confused. Sharon responded, "Well, you men should have said something to Fred—or to me—that he was screwing up. It could have saved him, not to mention the logs." The men responded that we were taught not to question what teachers told us to do even if it seemed wrong, cruel, or immoral. Sharon begged the question, growing more agitated, arguing that students should never blindly follow a teacher. This flew right in the face of the infallibility that Sharon, Fred, and the other teachers insisted upon—the slightest perceived criticism was met with attacks. And now she wanted us to shoulder the responsibility for not challenging Fred. There was no way to reconcile what Sharon was saying. I decided to make this a learning experience and go along with it.

Fred's involuntary departure was devastating. We loved him. We admired him. We looked up to him. His dismissal seemed random and arbitrary and severe. A couple of men on Retreat were so shattered by it that when we returned to New York, they never came back to School. Departures were like deaths to those who remained. For one, we would never see them again in class and we were forbidden from contacting them or taking their calls. It was said that once you left School, you lost your connection with the Work. Anyone who left was instructed to stop reading any of the books we studied. Even if you did not comply with that rule, it was said that the books were meaningless unless you were also connected with real teachers in a real school—i.e., "C Influence." C Influence is esoteric knowledge and can only be transmitted by teachers, not by a book.

Jimmy had only come to our class a couple of years before, but he seemed at home at the ranch. He was more relaxed around Sharon than Fred and the other teachers. The other teachers, including Robert, respected Jimmy. Fred had clearly botched the stripping job and was out of his element, but Jimmy was more knowledgeable about the physical ranch work. Unlike Fred, he got his hands dirty. He was our contemporary. It appeared that he was going to be Fred's replacement, and in fact he was. Classes taught by him were completely different. The harsh treatment we experienced from Fred was over: that was left to Sharon and Robert and Maude. Jimmy was brilliant, funny, and down to earth. He was like a peer. And he also played guitar.

Integrating

When we got back to New York that summer, Jimmy asked Seth, Peter, and me to start a band. I'd given up playing with the Blue Laws a couple of years earlier, mostly because I was too busy with School and could not make the rehearsals or gigs, but also because I wanted to spend more time pursuing artistic endeavors with my friends in Joshua's acting class. We called our new band, The Fellas. Jimmy was an excellent blues guitarist in the style of the Vaughan brothers. Seth was a talented writer and singer and played drums in addition to guitar. By day he was a producer. And Peter (a gallery owner by day) was also a gifted writer and singer who played piano. He was a tall, blond midwesterner and was kind and soft-spoken. Peter lived in a four thousand square foot loft in Brooklyn—the entire upstairs of a building that housed an auto shop on the ground floor. It was an ideal place for practicing. We gelled. All original music. Three excellent songwriters with different styles. The goodwill and camaraderie that we had were a big part of it. School made us close. And we got closer. "The Fellas" became my closest friends in and out of School.

We set up a recording studio in our rehearsal space with ambitions to record ourselves and possibly others. We invested in equipment and constructed a sound booth. We had standing rehearsals every Friday night, where we'd meet at Peter's in Greenpoint, get takeout Chinese fried chicken with fried rice and extra hot sauce, and then practice and record until 2:00 a.m. This was my Friday night for years. Sometimes we played all weekend. When we were not playing, we were socializing, sometimes going to Jimmy's home on Long Island. My School and out of School lives were beginning to blend.

There was a woman in class named Linda. She was tall, had dark brown eyes, long dark hair, and dressed urbanely, belying her New Mexico cowgirl background. She reminded me of a French girlfriend I had had in the 1980s. Maybe it was the fact that she was fluent in French, worked for Louis Vuitton, and they looked alike. I had a crush on her. Over the years, we got to be friendly. In 1995, I asked if she wanted to get together outside class, and she agreed. I asked Sharon's permission, and it was granted. It was a big deal for me. Although I'd had romantic relationships with a few other women inside and outside class in the past years, Linda was different because I wanted it to be serious.

I barely knew Linda, but we had School in common, and we thought that made up for really getting to know each other. I remembered Hazel's remarks on my first day about soul mates. Having approval from our teacher—the most important person in our lives—intensified things. The relationship moved quickly. We visited her family several times in New Mexico and she met my mother, Matthew, and sister-in-law Melissa, and some of my old friends. We spent almost every night together. In nine months we were engaged. It was exciting. It was fast. When people dated in School, the relationship was to be kept confidential from other students until Sharon decided it was time to make it public. When we got engaged, we announced it in class to well wishes and some surprise and some feigned surprise. I was thirty-five and wanted a family. This relationship promised to be different than any I could have with a woman outside School.

But after several months of engagement, Linda and I ran into trouble. I wasn't allowed to tell her about going to Montana for Retreat (per Sharon) and it drove her crazy that I simply disappeared for a week with only a vague excuse. When I did let her in on the secret, she was incensed that she hadn't been invited. But we tried to keep it together. Jimmy and Sharon, separately and outside class, asked about our relationship. Jimmy, who was now one of my closest friends, disliked Linda. Though Sharon had approved of our engagement, now she told me not to marry Linda. She felt that we didn't have "enough in common." She said it wouldn't "work out," and this persuaded me to break it off. Linda was relieved when we ended it. Sharon said—implying she had something or someone else in mind—"Spencer, there are other women better suited for you." Still, I was heartbroken and disappointed, believing that I wasn't destined to find a mate. I was pushing thirty-seven, which, according to Sharon, was an age by which it was "essential for a man to get married because of the celestial influences pouring down." I believed Sharon and Jimmy were in my corner.

Montana 1996 and the Bone

The ground surrounding Karnak was typical Montana: stubbornly rocky. There was a clearing to the south of Karnak where Sharon wanted us to dig a ten-by-twelve-foot hole, ten feet deep for a septic tank. In three days. It would have taken a machine half a morning to accomplish this feat but, again, Sharon wanted her students to perform this work so we could work on ourselves. Shovels alone were insufficient for the job. The ground needed to be loosened with pickaxes. There were eight men. We worked side by side for fourteen hours per day. "The Men's Project" was challenging, but with Jimmy as our leader, it was fun. The Fellas were all there, as were several other men I considered as close as brothers. It was serene in this clearing, deep in the woods at the foot of the snowcapped mountains and tall fragrant pine trees. Even the old dying trees had a certain dignity and purpose—like old soldiers who had spent their lives guarding the Queen. Eagles and hawks soared and the occasional black bear and deer came upon us, startled, and fled. The horses were close enough to hear their snorts and neighs. It was buggy but this year we had Ben's 100 DEET, which we slathered on. Direct sunlight made its way down to us in the clearing but in the surrounding dense forest shafts of light beamed like theater lights. And then there was the elevation: it was about 3,700 feet high, around three times higher than the Empire State Building.

Jimmy worked with us, not only teaching us how to use the tools but also taking turns to pick and dig. A pickax takes some getting

used to and can not only be ineffective but also dangerous. We therefore worked in shifts in the pit and were careful when swinging. The
Montana days were long and hot. But we were relaxed, joked, and
didn't constantly remind each other to remember ourselves or work
on ourselves. It didn't even feel like we were doing the Work. We
made time Aims to complete a certain depth within a certain period.
Exhausting but exhilarating, we were like a machine—a single cosmos interconnected and acutely aware of each other's movements
just as a person is aware of the tip of their head down to their pinky
toe. By the fourth day, it was clear we were going to make the Aim,
however, we decided we wanted to finish the job before the noon
meeting with Sharon.

That last hour was intense. We had been working in three groups
of four and taking turns, but we decided instead to work in two
groups of six because we were mostly digging and not pickaxing. We
were making progress, but it was getting tight. So for the last five minutes, Jimmy had eight of us work at a time, with four rotating in and
out of the ditch. We were pumped and loopy. Jimmy barked orders
and directed us with great precision. With about two minutes left,
George needed to use the pickax to loosen a rock, but in the rush, he
didn't warn the rest of us and nobody saw it. That was a mistake. On
his windup, over his shoulder, the blade smashed Brian in his lower
arm, shearing through straight to the bone, which was now visible.
Brian let out a ghastly scream, George rushed to him, and everyone
stopped what they were doing and helped Brian out of the ten-foot-
deep ditch. Yes, we had made the Aim.

We helped Brian out of the ditch and Jimmy brought over a
towel, which he wrapped around his arm. Brian's face was white,
and he was in shock. The hospital was an hour away in Kalispell. He
was bleeding, but not heavily, and Jimmy tied a tourniquet, a car was
brought over, and they sped off. We were also in shock, especially
George, who hit him. George wondered aloud about if he had swung
one split second sooner, he might have hit Brian in his skull, perhaps
killing him. We tried to calm George and left the site to head to the
meeting.

Sharon had been told about the incident before she'd come out for the meeting. She said that Brian would be fine. She assured us that in all the years and all the hundreds of projects that had been done on Retreat, nobody had been seriously injured.[23] "This is the Work. The Work has always protected School. That's why your connection to School is so important. We can discuss this more tonight when Brian comes back from Kalispell." We read a commentary and met for three hours.

Brian was back by dinner. His arm was in a cast and sling, and he looked better, albeit a little worn. The color had returned to his face. The only person brave enough to point out Sharon's nose job, he was not only unfiltered, but he was earnest, honest, and had a willingness to blame himself for all perceived negative events. This ability to take "the dirty end of the stick" distinguished advanced students from the less advanced. Those of us on Retreat were generally more advanced and therefore able to sustain the extended periods of time in which Sharon helped us see—with the Work—what it was in ourselves that caused negative events to happen to us. By this, we could take responsibility for our lives and begin to change. But this was hard work and required us to be open to accepting help from Sharon on identifying how we were to blame; Sharon was expert at pointing this out. And it was a "pressure cooker" as Fred often said. If a fellow student was temporarily unwilling to accept certain help, we were all encouraged to point it out, lest we be shirking our responsibilities as essence friends.

Our actions, inactions, character flaws, prior decisions, emotions, thoughts, and even simple gestures or facial expressions had enormous and direct implications on all events and circumstances in our lives,

---

23 This was false. Several people were seriously injured building the ranch, including one man who nearly died when a log smashed into his head, and another man who almost sliced off his arm with a chainsaw. Maude once fell off a horse at the ranch, suffering broken ribs and a punctured lung. Sharon publicly blamed her for the accident. At Alex Horn's urging, one man assaulted another student, requiring a visit to the emergency room for a broken jaw which needed to be wired. And then there was Brian's fracture and the psychological injuries Sharon and Alex inflicted for decades.

our wealth, our appearance, our relationships, the list goes on. Sharon also told us that illnesses were the result of our negative emotions; even cancer could be caused by negativity. Thus, by maintaining positive emotions, we could remain healthy.[24] Our fate was in our own hands.

So when the post-dinner meeting came that night, Sharon immediately spoke to Brian. She had already been briefed on his condition, but we had not. She asked him how he was feeling and whether he was in any pain. He said that he was feeling better but was taking strong pain medications. After some more back-and-forth he explained to the rest of us that the break was very serious and that it would take several months to correct. He also said that the doctors in Kalispell were excellent but that he would probably need surgery or surgeries when he got back to New York. He also said that he was lucky that the pickax hit him the way it did because if it had hit an artery he could have bled to death. The discussion then opened to other students expressing their relief that he wasn't more seriously hurt. Kim noted that it was because of the power of the Work that he was saved from something more serious. Some people spoke positively how this event could be a marker for Brian in terms of his evolution.

Sharon then asked Brian what he learned from the experience in terms of his being. Brian said that he was never much of a physical person, opting more for intellectual pursuits and that is why this happened. Sharon didn't buy it. "Brian, you are looking at this in the most outer way. You always look at the outer and not the inner. If you continue to be outer directed—caring about looking good or looking smart—you will ruin your life. You might even die. It's a matter of life and death." Everyone was sitting at the edge of their seats.

I had one of those moments where I took a stop to grasp the situation and my setting. What would an outside observer see, hear, and perceive if they were in the room? Here I was, sitting in an oversized log cabin with a large group of highly educated, intelligent friends, who were lucky enough to be in this beautiful and sacred place and have Sharon all to ourselves. Like Montana, Sharon was wild and

---

24 It never occurred to anyone to blame Sharon for her unhealthy habits such as chain smoking, substance abuse, and overeating.

unpredictable and fierce but this is where I belonged and wanted to be. The room was alive—the vivid colors, the smells of the dinner, the coffee percolating, the hunting trophies on the wall, the view of the majestic mountains out the window, the sun barely set at 10:00 p.m. It was like a dream, but it was real. I had the simultaneous understanding that nobody on the outside could possibly make sense of this.

Sharon said, "Brian, the reason this happened is because you were fast asleep and not awake. Sleep is so mechanical. Being awake takes a conscious effort and the only way for you to be awake is from the Work. Brian, why won't you take the Work seriously?" she asked rhetorically. She continued, "Brian, you are so identified with your job, with your wife and children, but pay no attention at all to your inner man, to your possibilities. You need to treat the Work like your one true love. For you, you need to make the Work your mistress." Everyone, especially Brian, was struck by that last remark. Sharon knew that Brian was dissatisfied in his sex life. She'd suggested over the years that Brian get a girlfriend on the side—but he never did. This time, Sharon was using the rather loaded mistress remark to prod Brian. It worked. Brian opened up. He said that he agreed that he had been asleep and that if he had been awake, he would not have been behind George when he swung the pickax. George disagreed, saying that obviously he was at fault because he swung the pickax. Sharon told George that he too was being "external" here and that he needed to think more "inwardly" and about the universe. "If you could see the invisible world and the dimensions of time and space, you and everyone else would have foreseen this event happening."

At this point, Seth brought up the bone. The day before Brian's accident, Seth and I had been walking together to the Guest House for breakfast. As we approached, he stopped and picked up a clean, white bone which was about a foot long and an inch in diameter. Although it was clearly the leg bone of an animal such as a deer or an elk, it resembled a human bone. It was on a busy footpath where we never saw an animal, so it was puzzling to us city folks how it got there. Seth brought it to the Guest House and left it on the picnic table just outside.

Now he told the group about the bone and went outside to retrieve it for us. He returned empty handed. "Sharon, it's gone!" Sharon took it in and spoke, "Seth, that bone was a sign from another dimension. You found that bone for a reason," pointing to Brian's arm. She continued to Seth, "You were absolutely correct in thinking about it, albeit after the fact. If you and Spencer had been awake and aware of the invisible world, you would have recognized that the bone was a presage of what happened to Brian."

It was an emotional day. We were spent. And now this revelation from Sharon: the entire room was rapt. Kim said that she felt tingles on her backbone. Seth concurred that he too felt an out-of-body experience. Peter was almost in tears. Tears welled up in my eyes—a combination of fear (this was spooky shit) and gratitude for learning this. Sharon's revelation seemed like deep wisdom which maybe I could invoke. I always saw connections in things that didn't seem to have a connection, but the bone just confirmed something for me: it seemed to wipe away the last shred of doubt I had about this group and all its secrets and omissions and deflections. Suddenly there was a new wave of love and kinship. People spoke about collective responsibility for each other. Women who had been cooking in the kitchen at the time of the accident pointed out that if they had been "remembering themselves" while the men were working in the ditch, perhaps this would not have happened. We were one-upping each other in trying to take responsibility and blame for Brian's misfortune. It even went so far that Raymond claimed that if he had not overslept, the "vibrations" for the day would have been better and prevented this incident. In hindsight, I now recall that the only person in the room who did not express any personal responsibility or blame for the event was Sharon.

The rest of this Retreat was festive, pleasurable. The petty acrimony, disputes, and conflict that often arose during our stressful daily work—and that were aired to Sharon's consternation during meetings—were absent for the rest of the Retreat. The men particularly felt a strong bond. The remaining projects were much easier, but we looked forward to working together, as a unit. The goodwill was abundant and permeated every single interaction. Brian was not able to do physical work and Sharon instructed him to spend his time reading and contemplating and "remembering himself." He spent much of the day in a wooden armchair facing the lake, reading, and smoking a pipe. When we went into town for the day off, he drove in Sharon's Jaguar with Jimmy and Sharon. At the meetings, Sharon reminded him that for him it was a matter of being "awake" and she reminded him to make the Work his mistress.

At the last commentary meeting, two students picked commentaries that Sharon liked, so she suggested someone flip a coin. I volunteered, the coin landing between two blades in the grass on its side. Sharon said it was a sign and that my commentary should be read. Seth said something about having a vision that I should be a teacher someday. Everyone looked at me in an approving way. Sharon and Jimmy were both smiling as if to say, "Yes, you could, just keep working on yourself."

This Retreat—and the kind of help Sharon was now giving us—was a reflection of how far we had come in the Work. Initially, Sharon's help consisted of advice on things like our jobs, love lives, and family lives. But now she was giving us commands or directions regarding a much deeper territory. That is—our minds, psychology, and how we looked at the world and ourselves.

I saw this as a positive and a privilege. We were now doing more "advanced work" because we had reached a higher level of apprenticeship. We were now deserving of Sharon's instructions, something we knew she wouldn't offer unless we were ready. By this time, and on this particular Retreat—what with the incident with Brian—we had experienced a collective deepening awe of Sharon and of her powers. We welcomed her entry further into our lives; it was an honor.

"Now, That Wasn't So Bad"

When it was over, he lit a cigarette, threw his head back against the pillow in satisfaction, and blew smoke rings. One, after another, slowly. My camp counselor Maury's tiny Lower East Side apartment was lit only by the yellow headlights of cars moving across the cracked wall. It was 3:00 a.m. It was freezing. I curled up against that wall, unable to sleep. I was fourteen. Mocking my resistance to his deed, Maury whispered, "Now that wasn't so bad, was it?" His second felony of the morning. Uttering these words, he implied my guilt, and he assaulted my thoughts, memories, and dreams, for what turned out to be nearly a lifetime.

The room smelled of reefer and Indian food from the all-night restaurant downstairs. I couldn't believe what I had done. It was repulsive. It was worse than getting punched in the face in the schoolyard. Yeah, it was his idea and he initiated it and I repeatedly said no no no no. But I finally did what he wanted me to do. And I *knew* he was bisexual, at least that is what he had told me—why was I there in the first place? I had been able to successfully repel him the last time I had slept over after he had taken me out to see Santana at the Academy of Music on East Fourteenth Street, some after-hours bar under the Queensboro Bridge, and *Deep Throat*. He gave me speed and we smoked a lot of pot. But this time I gave in, and I did what he wanted me to do. He had worn me down; I was tired and now I could get some sleep without his squirmy, fleshy, hairy, disgusting leg draped over me. Until now, I had never touched another person. Nobody. Why did it have to be with him? With a man, and not a girl? What was wrong with me?

I was humiliated. But it was my fault. I hadn't run away. This could only mean one thing: I was gay. I didn't realize I was gay. I was never attracted to boys. But I needed to confront this. I didn't know much about it, but I did think that being gay was a horrible fate, like some chronic disease.

The following evening I went with my mother and aunt to see *Fiddler on the Roof* at the Jones Beach Theater. I could barely face them. I was consumed with guilt. If my mother knew her fourteen-year-old son had been with a twenty-year-old man she would have been mortified. She might not even believe me: she knew Maury very well and liked him (whenever he called the house they always chatted first.) I could not possibly discuss this with anyone. I would just have to pretend I was straight and live a secret life and hope that my "homosexual tendencies" didn't get the best of me. And although I hated that sick fucking bastard for doing this to me, it was my own fault.

I was haunted by this night—this secret—for thirty-five years. A big part of me felt damaged and unwanted and worthless and ashamed. It had sowed doubt in my very identity. I had kept this secret until I chose to reveal it at Retreat to Sharon.

We were on her porch for a commentary meeting. Secluded, safe, and sleep deprived, it was the perfect atmosphere for divulging the most intimate and painful thoughts, feelings, and secrets among understanding family. A recurring theme this week seemed to be childhood traumas. Sharon had encouraged this—she said it was imperative in order to evolve. And so people were digging and digging into some horrible events; and then sexual traumas came up: Danny told us he had sex with another boy when he was fifteen; Ronald confessed to letting other boys kick his testicles; Sheila said her father had repeatedly raped her sister when she was younger. Sharon would dole out advice that seemed compassionate and constructive. It was safe. And I didn't want to miss this bus or be perceived as holding back or look like I wasn't working on myself. In this 24/7 School environment it was imperative to dig as deep as possible.

It was serene: clear big skies, snowcapped mountains, warm dry air, soaring eagles, buzzing mosquitoes, the aroma of DEET, and we existed in a state of semiconscious exhaustion. So I jumped in.

"I've never told anyone this Sharon, but it's coming up now."

Sharon looked straight at me, seated ten feet from me in the circle of chairs surrounding her outdoor recliner. Her expression was that of an inquisitive doctor, calm, confident, and ready for anything: she was an expert at eliciting secrets. Especially about sexual traumas.

"Sharon," I said, "When I was fourteen, I touched a camp counselor who was twenty. I was sleeping over at his apartment. He wanted to touch me, but I refused, however, I agreed to touch him instead. It was three in the morning. I could have refused it entirely, but I felt I had no choice. I could have left but I didn't. I have not been able to get over this event. It's been a source of a lot of pain that I brought this on to myself. It has led me to question my own identity. What in my being caused this?"

Sharon didn't bat an eye. She asked no questions. She jumped in with complete assuredness, speaking calmly but clinically, as if she had heard this exact issue a million times before, and generously dispensed her wisdom, "Spencer, it's OK, it really is, and I want you to stop—stop today, as of this moment—stop thinking about this entirely. You can do that. Just stop."

I was relieved. And then she dispensed this nugget of wisdom, "Children experiment all the time with sex. You were experimenting. That's all. It is perfectly normal to experiment with the same sex." And then she normalized it even more, "It's also perfectly normal to experiment with an older boy. So you must stop thinking about this. Will you, Spencer?" I stared at Sharon, in sort of in a daze, and promised her I would.

I was feeling better knowing that this was nothing more than a one-time "experiment" rather than an acting out of a "homosexual tendency." This was normal behavior on my part. And although she agreed that I was responsible for what happened to me, it wasn't worth thinking about. In fact Sharon was pretty clear with everyone who mentioned these traumas that they were not things to dwell on. Although she did scold Sheila for not reporting her father to the police and indicated that Sheila's mother must have known about it. "Another girl would have stopped the father, but you did not and are responsible for what was done to your sister."

My Friend the Dancer

In the Fall of 1996—just after Linda and I broke up—Seth invited me to bring my bass to a dance studio and help him accompany two dancers—his wife, Sara, and a woman named Beth, another student. Beth had recently been invited back to School by Sharon, years after Sharon had kicked her out. Beth rarely spoke about herself in class, so I didn't know much about her. But when she did speak—about the Work ideas—she was articulate and insightful. Beth carried herself like the dancer she was: graceful and deliberate.

Seth's melodic and personal songs were well-suited for the kind of dance Beth was choreographing. It combined classical and modern elements that were elegant and profound. Both women were over forty and the themes revolved around rediscovery and renewal. Eventually, the project gathered steam and they were able to persuade Sharon to allow other classmates to work on it together. When Sharon came to visit a rehearsal, she was impressed with what she saw and announced on the spot that she was going to direct it and produce a dance concert.

At about this time, Sharon called me over after class. She put her hand on my shoulder and pulled me closer. The smell of vodka on her breath was strong as she whispered in my ear, "Think about getting together with Beth. You would be perfect together."

In rehearsals, I came to see Beth as talented, sensitive, and ambitious. The four of us—Seth, Sara, Beth, and I—began socializing after rehearsals. When Seth and Sara's son was born, they asked Beth and me to become his godparents. I picked up Beth in my car on the corner of Twenty-third Street and the FDR to go to Brooklyn for the naming ceremony. That was the first time we were alone. We had a good connection: we loved School, the Work, Sharon, our common friends, and creating the dance concert. We started to hang out together, just the two of us, for drinks and dinner. She had other children from a previous marriage. When I told Sharon I wanted to date Beth, she was ecstatic and told me, "You will love Beth's children, they are exactly like her."

I was almost thirty-seven, the age by which Sharon expected us to be married. Sharon asked me how things were going with Beth and whether we were serious. Even though I wasn't very attracted to her physically (and she wasn't very attracted to me), I started to think that maybe she could be the School soul mate Hazel had wished for me and that—through the Work—the physical attraction would grow over time. I also wanted to please Sharon, who knew what was best. Within months, Beth and I got engaged. Sharon was thrilled. The whole School was thrilled. Beth knew that I wanted my own child and even though she was forty-two, she agreed. Within months, we were married. Sharon and Robert came to our wedding along with dozens of School friends. My mother and Matthew were there along with a handful of my close cousins, but none of my old college or high school friends like Vicki, David, or Colin were invited. Although Matthew and my mother had only met Beth a couple of times before the wedding, it was the first time my mother and Matthew had ever seen Sharon or any of my School friends. My family never asked me who all these strangers were or where my old friends were; I just told them they were friends from my "acting class." Although Matthew, as the best man, gave the toast, Sharon stood right next to Beth and me as he spoke—glowing—visibly showing her importance in our marriage. She also sat at the head table with our parents. My School and family worlds collided briefly, and it was surreal.

Beth and I spent our honeymoon at Jimmy's house in Long Island. I moved into Beth's apartment with her teenage children. At the wedding Sharon said to me, "Now you have the family you always wanted." I was now in a School marriage.

During our engagement, Beth told me that Peterson (another teacher whom Beth had briefly dated) had previously been married to Hazel and that the two of them had three children before divorcing. Fred and Priscilla were also married and had three children. After both couples got divorced, Fred married Hazel. It was interesting to know that if a School marriage didn't work out, Sharon would find another relationship with another student. This is what had happened to me in fact: breaking up with Linda and getting married to Beth within months. Indeed, the Work had a way of finding your soul mate.

Late one afternoon in the winter of 1998, while I was driving north on the FDR service road toward East Thirty-fourth Street, my cell phone chirped. I looked down. It was from a blocked number. "Spencer." It was Sharon. "Hi Sharon," I said, my pulse quickening as it did anytime she called me. Sharon never called to schmooze or just say hello; there was always an agenda and in fact not once did she ever even say hello when she called. She got right to the point. She announced, "I don't like the idea of Beth getting pregnant at her age. It's potentially dangerous. The child could have Down syndrome and you would have to put it up for adoption." I protested, something I could sometimes—sometimes—do when speaking one-on-one with Sharon. I reasoned that it was safe and that Beth wanted to get pregnant. "No, Spencer, what you should do is to impregnate Hannah, she can carry the baby, and you and Beth can raise the baby as your own." Hannah was Beth's nineteen-year-old daughter. I couldn't process what I was hearing. I said, "Are you serious, Sharon?" She responded, "Of course. I'm sure Hannah would be happy to do this. She's still young. She would do it for you." I told her I didn't think it would be a good idea, hoping Sharon would relent. She just dropped it. She never brought it up again.[25]

I had mixed feelings about relating this to Beth. On one hand, Beth worshipped (and feared) Sharon. Part of me didn't want to burst her bubble. But this was such an outrageous thing, and Beth needed to know it. So I told her when I got home. Beth didn't say a word, the blood left her face, she closed her eyes, and shook her head in disbelief. She was on the verge of tears. We never discussed it again.

Sharon was suggesting that I engage in incest to conceive a child. This child would be the grandchild of my wife, the child of my stepdaughter, and the niece or nephew of my other stepchildren. It was repugnant and I never considered it for a second. But I did overlook it. Not because I thought Sharon was demented but because I thought, in my compromised condition, that Sharon was a free spirit—uninhibited and unconstrained from all conventions—and that someone of her "hippie mindset" would of course recommend this. I gave her a pass. A big one.

There is a syndrome called folie à plusieurs (or "folly of several") in which two or more people (usually family members) share the same delusional beliefs or hallucinations that are transmitted between them. These usually involve paranoid delusions and have resulted in murder, self-harm, and even financial crimes. In 2008, an Indian family of eleven hanged themselves in their home with the apparent belief that they would be saved from death at the last moment by a "superpower." The police indicated that the family might have been suffering from shared psychotic disorder. It was speculated by employees of Theranos—the Silicon Valley start-up that failed spectacularly just before its leaders were indicted for securities fraud—that the two leaders of the company were suffering from shared delusional ideas that the phony blood-testing product they were developing actually worked. I've wondered whether many of us in School were suffering from Sharon's delusions, paranoias, and perversions. This might explain a lot of what many students experienced, believed, and agreed to do.

---

25 In 1999, Beth gave birth to our healthy son.

Georgia on My Mind

In the fall of 1997, after our wedding, about a dozen members of School and Sharon traveled to Tbilisi, Georgia, to perform Beth's dance concert in a festival. I was there to play in the band that accompanied the dance. Lianne Klapper, a student of School and a documentarian, came along to make a film about a nearby orphanage. Sharon decided to accompany Lianne along with Peter who was there playing with the band. (Peter was an orphan himself.)

On the last night of our dance concert performance, Sharon invited the festival organizer, a Georgian woman named Natia, to see our performance. Natia was in her early sixties and had been a well-known and popular actress in her country. Reveling in the country's newfound freedom and ability to mount art without censorship or control, she was a courageous and strong woman who had managed to attract hundreds of performers from around the world to perform there. Natia came to our performance, but because she had to see several other shows that evening, she left after the first act. When Sharon found out that Natia had left, she was enraged. When Natia learned that Sharon was upset, she returned to the theater after the show to find Sharon and her entourage backstage. As Natia entered, Sharon started to wail. Loudly. And scream. More like a shriek. At Natia. "How dare you insult us by leaving in the middle of the performance." Natia quickly apologized, saying that while she loved the performance and wanted to stay she was obliged as the organizer to drop by the other performances.

Sharon wasn't placated. "You are an ungrateful host,[26] and we will never ever come back to this shithole again," Sharon roared. "What kind of person are you to invite us and disrespect us?" All the while Sharon was in tears and her most fervent allies—Hazel and Christopher, a teacher and actor who attended the trip—were sitting right next to her, glaring at Natia, and looked about to jump her.

Natia was flabbergasted. But she was also an actress. She started to cry and beg for forgiveness. But to her—and everyone's—horror, this only made Sharon more enraged, using Natia's contrition as an admission of guilt and continuing her tirade. Hazel and Christopher—in a sickening display of blind loyalty to Sharon—joined in, railing at Natia for her "disrespect." But most of us were appalled and embarrassed. Seth got up and walked out into the back of the theater. So did I. I couldn't wait for it to end. Soon, Natia left in shambles. The group sat in silence. We never saw her again.

Sharon spoke in a quivering voice as though she'd just survived an assassination attempt. "What she did was unforgivable—to invite us and disrespect us. She treated us like shit. Yet, I tried to help her by giving it to her straight—by giving her a shock. But she was completely cut off from the help." At this point Christopher chimed in, "Sharon, thank you for trying to help her and thank you for giving us the privilege of witnessing you trying to help her. I was witnessing 'Conscious Anger.'" Sharon agreed, "Yes you did." And several people nodded their heads. I couldn't reconcile my disgust and embarrassment with my allegiance to Sharon, so—as I usually did—I just ignored it and worked on myself. We returned to New York shortly thereafter.

---

26 The Georgians couldn't have been better hosts. Although Sharon stayed in a hotel, the rest of us were housed for free in the homes of locals who were warm and lovely. They cooked us meals and made us feel comfortable. Everyone was assigned young women who were our ever-present interpreters and guides. Everyone was given the equivalent of $200 in spending cash. Transportation was provided. We were treated like celebrities.

Driving Ms. Sharon and Date Night

After Beth and I got married, Sharon asked me to do the honor of driving her to and from class. By now, her class visits were weekly. I would pull up to her building on West Twelfth Street between Fifth and Sixth Avenues and wait for her to come downstairs. Standing by her front door, she would hug me and kiss my cheek, hook her arm through mine and slowly walk as I guided her to the passenger seat. She always had the faint smell of a woodsy perfume with a nose of talcum powder. She would lean her full weight on my arm. For such a formidable and dominating person, she was unsteady and helpless—a juxtaposition to the power she held over the hundreds of others in her orbit. I was alone with someone nearly on par with Buddha. She had all the answers, the powers. With her, anything was possible. And because of her supernatural powers and intellect, I always felt safe and protected with her. So I looked forward to these drives, to having her to myself. Other students would have killed to have this alone time with Sharon. Also, on these drives she was predictably pleasant, charming, and in good spirits. The conversations tended to be about current events or movies, theater, or anything else she wanted to speak about. I got the feeling she wanted to be off-duty.

But sometimes we spoke about me. Once she suggested that I go by "S. Lee Schneider." She said it sounded more "lawyerly, like F. Lee Bailey." Once she told me to get into trusts and estates law because the clients are either "rich or dead." She told me I would make a "killing" investing in health food restaurants. Once, when I drove her to the airport she told me not to use the E-Z Pass lane. She said she did not want the government to know where she was going. Driving Sharon made me special and privileged, even over teachers—I sensed their jealousy when we walked out of the classroom at the end of the night. Sometimes after classes, she would talk to me about other students, invariably women, usually in a disparaging way. "Barbara is so asleep and is ruining her life with that husband of hers—she needs to divorce him." "Karen is in self-will." "Linda needs to get fucked more often." On more than one occasion in the car, and on the phone, she disparaged Beth to me. She complained that Beth was too "cerebral" and knew the Work on paper but not in her "being." She asked me about how things were at "home" and whether Beth was acting "off." She often let me in on her secrets while driving: how she met Alex, how she dated her first cousin, what it was like to be a young actor in the 1960s with two small children, her friendships with celebrities (Meryl, Bobby, Paul, John, Ringo, Frank, Mia).

In the summer of 1998, when Beth was pregnant, Sharon forbade her (as she did with many pregnant women) from flying in an airplane, and therefore Beth did not come to Retreat that summer. This Retreat—like the last two—no longer involved heavy-duty construction or demanding physical work. Now we engaged in projects such as painting or staining the dozen log cabin structures, making minor repairs, and performing light maintenance of her ranch.

When Sharon decided to have a day off from the ranch, she asked me to drive her to Kalispell a little earlier than the rest of the group so that I could take her to the dentist. When we got in the car, Sharon told me that Bruce Springsteen had "jammed" the night before at some venue where her daughter had seen him in New York. Her daughter, whom I knew only in passing, had been a student briefly and was in a marriage arranged by Sharon to another student. Nothing else was memorable about that trip except that, as usual, the drive was beautiful. And like all my drives with her in the car, sitting side by side, whether in the mountains of Montana or valleys of New York, I didn't want the drive to end. So I drove slowly to cherish each minute with my teacher.

In addition to the ranch, Sharon had a house in Kalispell, which we referred to as the "K House," and I took her there after her dentist appointment. She said that she wanted me to stay over at her house that night in one of the guest rooms down the hall from her room, but first, she wanted to go to see a movie that evening. The movie she chose to see was *The Truman Show*, about a boy who was adopted and raised by a corporation and who lives in a reality TV show revolving around his life; he eventually discovers the truth and decides to escape.

As we got out of the car at the movie theater, Sharon put her hand on my arm and I understood, with discomfort, that we were on a date. I bought our tickets, some popcorn, Cokes, and we watched the movie from the last row. Sharon loved it and considered it an allegory to the Work because it also dealt with emerging from a state of sleep and realizing the need to escape. That night I slept at Sharon's house in the guest room down the hall.

While I was at Sharon's house, the rest of the students and teachers were staying overnight in a motel. The following day I joined them for a whitewater rafting excursion near Glacier Park. At the end of the long day of rafting, I went back to Sharon's house, to chauffeur her back to the ranch. It was tough to head back to the ranch after these overnight trips to town: there was more work to be done and more pressure. But on the drive back with Sharon she told me that she thought I had the ability "to do anything I wanted." She repeated this at the meeting the next day in front of everyone. It was a moment I didn't forget. There was nothing like getting praise from Sharon. Nobody I knew did it better. And nobody could tear you down to pieces like Sharon.

PART 4
2000–2009

The sense of discovery, personal empowerment, community, and security I experienced in the previous decade turned into loss, monotony, and fear. I'd become dependent upon School in an unhealthy way, isolated from the rest of my friends and family, and my life was controlled by Sharon Gans and others. Like former junkies say, the best high is the first one; for me the best years of School were the first ones. The moments of chaos and abuse that we occasionally witnessed that first decade became de rigueur as the years progressed— Sharon sank deeper into her mental disease and drug and alcohol abuse. We also suffered the departure of close friends, a crazy tumult in which Sharon thrived, the deterioration of our mental and physical health, and watched as Sharon built and tore down friendships and even families—including mine. The secret history and truth of School—and who Sharon and Alex really were—was revealed, courtesy of the internet. By the end of the decade, I was a wreck.

"Time May Change Me"

When other students left School, it was like they were losing their minds or—like Hiram Cosby or my childhood friend Kenny—killing themselves. We understood that if you left School—aside from losing your teachers—you would lose the Work and all it provides. You lose your protection. You lose safety. You lose the invisible world. And you lose your friends. When people left, they were dead to us; and in the event we saw them on the street we were to run the other way; if they contacted us, we were to shut it down; they were killer zombies. Obviously, in no circumstances were we to contact them.

When George decided to leave, it came as a sudden blow to me, Seth, and Peter, because the four of us were very close from Retreat, acting class, and going out occasionally. Similar to the Fellas, our friendship transcended School. Unlike 90 percent of the people in School, we would have been friends had we met outside School. George had just gotten married, and wanted to spend more time with his wife.

But when Seth left, it was more disruptive because of how close Beth and I were with him and his wife. The four of us had been inseparable before and after the trip to Georgia. When their son was a toddler, Seth and I would take him out together for Saturday mornings. Once we were in the old Sam Ash store on West Forty-eighth

Street taking turns playing guitars and watching his son. So equally attentive were we to his son that Seth and I joked that we looked like a same-sex couple. One night over dinner at the Knickerbocker on University Place with Sara, Beth, and me, Seth announced that he was planning to leave School. It hurt the three of us. It was like we were breaking up. He hadn't told anyone of his decision, even his wife. He said that he was being stifled in his artistic life. We tried to talk him out of it, telling him that the connection to School would help him achieve that goal. It didn't work. He could not recover after witnessing Sharon's cruelty to Natia in Georgia. This dinner was the last time I saw him. When he left, Sharon pressured Sara to get divorced. She did. Sara remained in School, but not for long.

Seth's departure broke up The Fellas. We continued on for a time without him, but we had played so many of his songs and we could not replace him. The center could not hold, and soon Peter left not only the band but also School. One day, he just disappeared. I was bereft. To make matters worse, after these friends left, there was no funeral, no wake, no shivah, and nobody talked about it. Those wounds festered, never really healing. I was also torn myself as to who would or could replace them in my life.

By the fall of 1999, School's attention was diverted to the pressing urgency of "Y2K." When the millennium came at midnight on December 31, 1999, every imaginable horror would befall civilization as we knew it: the utility infrastructure would collapse, leaving everyone in darkness and unable to conduct even the most basic of life-supporting activities. There would be shortages of food and water and likely mass riots. Satellites would fall to the earth and potentially nuclear rockets would accidentally launch. It promised to be a real shitshow.

I had been intrigued by all the news yet was skeptical that anything major would come of it. But Sharon and School saw it differently. While Sharon didn't predict exactly what would happen, she was warning that something terrible would. She said that everything would be different after Y2K, but that it was lucky we were in School because we would "cross this interval" together. She told people to stock up on essentials such as water and canned goods. It wasn't a recommendation: it was help, which meant that we needed to do this for our inner development. People panicked. I remember Kim, who had a country house upstate, was buying enough food and water to exist for a year and had installed a solar-powered generator. Kim, I should add, was a smart woman, and her husband was also a highly educated man, so I was astonished that she had gone to such lengths. For our part, Beth and I complied with the instruction by purchasing two large water cooler bottles from Costco as well as three large tins of tuna fish, a giant jar of peanut butter, and two boxes of Triscuit crackers (all which were eventually donated to a food pantry).

One night in class, in December 1999, one of the teachers from Boston came to lead. Josiah was a college professor, brilliant and funny. He wore wire-rim glasses and had a warm smile and easygoing demeanor. But he was pretty wired up this night. The topic was Y2K. We were discussing how this event could prove to be the end of the world as we knew it. The class devolved into rampant speculation and discussions about things with which nobody in the class had any expertise. At one point, I raised my skepticism with Josiah, feeling that my point was important and that he would be reasonable. "I promise you that the power grid will go down. In fact I guarantee it," he rebuked me. I never said a single thing about Y2K again in class.

For the big night, Sharon made us all go up to School's upstate weekend compound. This compound had been financed, purchased, and then built with the hands of over a hundred members of School over a couple of years. Working through the night on weekends in dangerous conditions—like Retreat—nobody was paid for their work. But those who didn't go to Montana in the summer with Sharon would have these weekend retreats through the winter months with her upstate. Sharon would preside over late-night meetings. On New Year's Eve 1999, there were about fifty of us at the main house upstate. We prepared a great dinner, danced, and celebrated the dawning of the new millennium with dance music still blaring and lights still on at 12:00:01. Y2K was never mentioned again in class or by anyone else in School.

Jim asked Sharon if I could represent him in negotiating his office lease; Raymond's company needed me to sue a contractor; Joni needed me to help her negotiate an exit package from her job; then there was Carl, who was renewing a lease for his medical practice. Sharon required that any kind of out-of-class relationship had to be approved. She agreed to each of these arrangements. They were all good clients, and I enjoyed representing them. And then there was Andre Podonok, another student.

Podonok was an émigré from Russia. He had moved to New York for college, worked hard, and struck it rich in real estate. A savvy developer, he had a big vision and big ego (he always put his name on his buildings). Podonok stood no more than five feet, five inches, but thought he was seven feet, five inches—he managed to emanate an imposing aura, full of bravado. Always dressed impeccably, he wore custom-made Italian suits and a pink tie with his company logo: it was his trademark look. He had a thick Russian accent, a shock of blond hair, and was missing his right pinky. I found him simultaneously repulsive and irresistible.

In 2000, Podonok asked Sharon for permission to hire me. She consented. We met over lunch at his club. He wanted me to help him with a new business he was opening that would buy distressed real estate. He said he admired my skills. I liked his intelligence and fairness. I signed on. We succeeded on the first deal. And the next one, and then the next one. Within a short course his business went from a value of less than $1 million to over $1 billion by dint of these wins and his ability to attract new investors with this track record. And in no time Podonok became one of my biggest and most lucrative clients. We also became friends. He was lonely and self-centered and the only joy in his life seemed to come from his job. Not unlike Sharon herself. The work we did was exciting, and we worked well together. Sharon was happy for both of us, telling me that Podonok "used the ideas of the Work in his business—that is why he does so well." Another teacher told me that "Podonok and you will make a lot of money."

Sharon Nights, Part III

Sharon held twice annual "Men's Meetings" and "Women's Meetings," all-night affairs to allow for uncensored conversations without the opposite sex. Sharon would preside along with Jimmy.

On this night, Sharon opened by telling us that although she was born a woman, because she had worked on herself so much, she knew exactly what it was like to "have a cock." Andrew spoke first. He revealed that he was not content with the quality of oral sex that his wife performed. Sharon suggested she practice more often and that in the meantime Andrew should get himself a "a young girl who you could jog with and get head from." James admitted that his wife Lori (who was also in School) and he were fighting a lot. Sharon told him to go home so that "you two lovebirds can fuck this out." One man spoke about having erectile dysfunction disorder. Sharon suggested that before trying Viagra, he go to a high-priced escort and try to "just relax." I was put off by how Sharon spoke like a sailor because it seemed so gratuitous and lascivious; but I figured that she did it intentionally to shock us out of our collective "morality" about sex.

It was a miracle. After storming out of class three years ago, Marcie was back. And on this night she had brought along her nine-month-old son. Sharon was there. We had a celebration. Gifts, balloons, tears of joy, toasts, testimonials about the power of the Work, gratitude to Sharon. We had never seen Marcie so happy. No explanation was given, but it was implied that she had conceived her son without the aid of any fertilization methods. It was not uncommon for women to bring their infants to class. The last woman in class who was pregnant was Patti, but she had left School over a year ago before she'd had her child. That was the last we'd heard of her.

When Beth and I came home after Marcie's return to class, Beth told me that Marcie's baby was Patti's son. Marcie had adopted him. Patti hadn't wanted to have the child, but Sharon didn't want her to abort, so Sharon arranged for the adoption.

I learned that night and over the course of the next few years that Sharon had arranged for several adoptions among students. Some of the children were never told about their adoptions. Sometimes Sharon convinced certain parents of newborns that they could not be "good parents," and told them to give up their children for adoptions, which she arranged with students or people outside School. Sometimes when married men had affairs with other women students and got them pregnant, the child would be raised by the unmarried woman, but Sharon would tell the cuckolded wife to be a good "stepmother" to the child. Sometimes a single mother student would be married off to another student and the child would be told that the man was their father, the biological father never being informed of the child's existence. It was all very confusing and hush-hush.

The following week there was another surprise celebration: Bob, a banker, and Carol, a designer, had gotten engaged. We had cake, champagne, gifts, toasts, the usual School celebration. But what wasn't usual was that up until that evening we knew Bob as Alice's husband and we knew Carol as Ted's wife. And we also knew both couples to be happy, but that Sharon didn't like these matches. Ted was a student in the other class, but Alice was in our class making it especially awkward. There had been a rumor going around that Sharon was so enchanted by Carol (from a wealthy family) that she offered her "any man she wanted" and she picked Bob. And yet, this night, here was Alice leading the celebration. She brought out the balloons and serenaded the happy couple with "Here, There and Everywhere." Alice was an amazing young woman: talented, smart, and a kind soul. And Sharon was so proud of Alice celebrating the wedding of her former husband and father of their children. Sharon said, "You are embodying 'Conscious Love,' Alice. Setting your husband free to pursue what he needs for his life. You have taken a big step in transforming your jealousy. Congratulations." As we gave Alice an ovation, the tears streamed down, unable to hide her humiliation.

I remember another night which, like so many, started well but progressed poorly. We could tell that Sharon was drinking more than usual and she was getting tired and when she drank more than usual and got tired, she could get peevish. Marie brought in work about her daughter Clara who was fifteen and having trouble in school and making friends. Sharon waved her hand and said, "I've heard this problem from you too much. The girl is a rotter, plain and simple. Send her to boarding school and send the bill to your ex-husband." Next, Carlene stood up and said her twin brother was asking to spend time with her and had questions about her "Tuesday and Thursday" evenings. Sharon instructed Carlene to cease all communications with her brother. And then Peggy said her eighty-year-old parents who lived in assisted living were also pestering her to visit: Sharon told her to stop seeing them.

Getting Out of Dodge

In the summer of 2000, gray smoke from forest fires choked the air out West. We smelled it as soon as we deplaned in Kalispell. Within twelve hours of our arrival at the ranch, Sharon called an end to the Retreat. It had nothing to do with the forest fires.

The trouble started the first morning. Without warning. We were assembled silently, serenely on the porch behind the Main House, awaiting our teacher's arrival. The morning rain giving way to the aroma of smoke and the Douglas firs. Hawks screeched overhead. Every prior year on the porch—the faces of friends, their obstacles, the help given by Sharon, the miracles—were merged in my mind and were present that moment. Upon Sharon's arrival, we stood. She smiled and waved faintly. She looked tired, in pain. Jimmy helped her into her recliner. She pushed back and sort of zoned out for a couple of minutes, and instead of asking about the commentary for the day, inquired with an edge, "Who cleaned my house this morning?" Kim and Beth answered that they had. "It looks like shit. What the hell is going on here with you?" Kim and Beth, Sharon's most loyal students who would do anything for her, looked like they'd been slapped. Sharon turned to Marion, who was with her husband, Harvey, and asked "Are you two fighting again?" Marion answered that they hadn't been, although it was known that they had recently gotten through some rough times. Sharon replied, "You two should be fucking, not fighting, or you should get divorced." Marion was shaking. Sharon plunged further, "Get over it, Marion, so your husband is fucking another woman—get over it." Marion got up and left the meeting. Sharon said, "Harvey, go to your wife." I sat three seats from Sharon, and I could feel her unexplained rage boiling over. I'd never seen her so persistently on the attack, especially at her most loyal students. She didn't look well, either. Her voice was strong, but her face was puffy, and her eyes seemed dull and empty. She signaled Jimmy to help her up. As she stood to go back into her house she said, "You're all asleep," and left us.

Jimmy and I followed her to find out what was wrong. She stopped and looked at us, the whites of her eyes bloodshot. "Retreat is now over. Everyone must leave." I said, "But Sharon, we just arrived, please don't do that." She replied, "Jimmy, the only people here awake are you and Spencer. I cannot work with anyone else." Jimmy tried to calm her down and she agreed to come back to the meeting. But when she returned to the porch, she stood behind her chair and said, "Retreat is now over. You haven't been working on yourselves and don't deserve Retreat." She scanned the room and said, "The only people I want to work with are Jimmy, Patrice, Sara, Spencer, and Norma. Everyone else, you are not to attend meetings with us nor have meals with me and the others. You will do all the cleaning and projects. Keep your own counsel." And with that Sharon left the porch.

Dejected. Shattered. Heartbroken. Some of the women were crying. Hazel was practically tearing her hair out. Then, one by one we trailed away from the porch, returning to our cabins. Beth was a complete wreck. For her it raised memories of when Sharon kicked her out of School. I couldn't console her. She was also angry that I had been selected to be on Retreat without her. I told her I would gladly leave with her at that moment. She wouldn't hear of it. This was tearing us up. I let her be and walked over to speak with Kim. We sat on the steps to her cabin. She was sobbing uncontrollably. She revealed to me that she had been having an ongoing affair with Harvey, the husband of Marion, her best friend, and that she had slept with another married student. I visited others who were equally devastated. Mark, who was a consultant, was walking down the road when I caught up with him—"My teacher sees failings in me, and I need to work on myself." The people who were in the Off Group blamed themselves. But our interconnectedness, over so many years, was deep. The only person who could interfere with our connection was Sharon. And now she was inexplicably fucking with it.

Jimmy was especially conflicted. Only a few of us knew that he was Sharon's son; I had learned about it a few years before when he confided in me. Jimmy feared that this Retreat could have serious consequences for School. Sharon had commanded that each group essentially ignore the other. We ate meals separately (the On Group with Sharon in her home and the Off Group in the Guest House). The Off Group continued to do all the cooking and cleaning and projects and were like zombies. Beth hardly spoke to me.

On the last night, the On Group was sitting in Sharon's home at her long dining room table waiting for her to come out of her room to join us. She was late. It had been an awful week. Patrice looked at the table and said out loud, "I don't know about the rest of you, but I think it's time to get the hell out of Dodge." It was like the spell had been broken. I felt that with this group of friends—also out from under the spell of Sharon—I could move on and get out.

But then, suddenly, Sharon walked in through the side door of the house. She shouted, "Surprise!!!! They are back. They woke up. The Work works." Behind her, in a single file were Harvey, Marion, Beth, Mark, Hazel, Kim, and the others. They were not nearly as cheerful as Sharon; they more resembled condemned prisoners who had just been given last-minute reprieves from the governor. All of us in the On Group similarly feigned happiness.

We left the next morning, driving to the airport, silently, in two vans. We couldn't get out of Montana soon enough. But when we arrived at the airport in Kalispell, we fell into each other's arms, comforting each other. We talked. We tried to digest what had happened. It became apparent that instead of breaking us up, Sharon's behavior seemed only to just bring us all closer together, united not in devotion to her but in anger.

In fact we were livid. Retreat had been brutal. We had talked on the plane, then over the phone for the first forty-eight hours after getting home. It was unanimous. Two nights later, we met at Jimmy's house in Brooklyn for our annual post-Retreat meeting to discuss our "reentry." But this was not going to be an ordinary meeting. Sharon had no idea how angry and bitter people were about the Retreat. She must have assumed that with the phony reunion on the last night, all would be forgiven. She had miscalculated. For one, Harvey and Marion were not at the meeting, and it was assumed—because nobody could get in touch with them—that they had left School; they had.

Everyone in that room had come to the independent conclusion that it would be impossible to stay in School another day. Sharon's behavior indicated that she might have had some kind of mental breakdown. We had heard that she had acted with similar brutality to the two other groups, including to her most trusted students, and Robert (who she publicly upbraided and who was said to have gotten violently ill as a result).[27] The only question was how we would leave and what we would do to study the Work after we left. Because although we were entirely disgusted with Sharon, we all still had a deep love of the Work. Sharon called Jimmy's house while we were meeting and even asked to get on the phone with some of us. We pretended that everything was fine. Sharon usually didn't return from Montana until October, so we had time to plan our next step.

We did not reach any plans that night but we agreed that the time had come to establish a new independent group to study the Work with Jimmy and perhaps others as leaders. We would also seek to recruit other members of School. In the days that followed we were consumed with meetings, lunches, and calls. Plans were beginning to jell. Sharon called me during these days to see how I was doing. We spoke about Al Gore's recent selection of Joe Lieberman as his running mate and Sharon indicated that she thought it was a brilliant

---

27   We had also learned that Sharon had discovered before our Retreat that her daughter's husband (who was also a student) had just been caught having an affair with a man; this should not have come as a total surprise because Sharon and her daughter knew he was gay.

pick. I felt guilty for pretending everything was all right as I was about to betray her, but I was still angry at her and disillusioned.

Beth and I agreed: we were going to leave, but we wanted to hear the collective plan—we wanted an exit strategy and to know that we would land with our friends. But before any cohesive plan could be devised, something unexpected happened. In the second class after we were back, Jimmy walked into class and announced, "Sharon and Robert are not my teachers anymore. I do not believe that they represent the ideas of the Work. I will be leaving School to study independently, and I welcome anyone here to come with me." Jimmy spoke for a few more minutes and left.

Having thrown down the gauntlet, Jimmy now expected the rest of us to join him. Some left immediately. About a dozen students from other classes left as well. But for others it wasn't so simple. I wanted to leave immediately, but Beth worked for another student who remained devoted to Sharon and knew she would lose her job if she left School. Although highly accomplished in her field, Beth had bought into the idea drilled into us by Sharon that she would not be able to find another job outside School. This was one of the crippling aspects of School—the ingrained belief that you could only thrive professionally (or personally) through the Work and affiliation with School. Similarly, I wasn't going to leave School without Beth, because I knew Sharon would sabotage our marriage. Each of these School relationships had Beth and me (and many others) handcuffed as Sharon's prisoners. Our escape plan was going nowhere. I watched as friends left and I was being left behind. Now with Jimmy gone and the exodus having begun, something else happened: Sharon got involved.

The following day she called everyone who had been on Retreat and told us that Jimmy was her son, that he had basically lost his mind, and that she loved us; she then asked us how we were doing. I was out of town on business for Podonok and she and I spoke only briefly, and I lied, telling her I was fine. Jimmy also called me and pressed me to leave and join him. I couldn't commit because I wanted to make a joint decision with my wife. Plus there was Podonok: I didn't want to lose his new business. I knew that if I left, we would be done, and, like Beth, I was concerned that I could not replace him. Jimmy was angry with my hesitancy. But leaving was more complicated than I had realized. I did not hear from him again.

Beth and I were still torn but decided to go to class the next night. Robert had come in from Boston to do damage control. It was somber. He explained that Jimmy had lost his mind and that nobody should contact him. Robert solicited people's views and thoughts and most expressed sadness and disappointment but overall reaffirmed their commitment to School and the Work and Sharon. After class, however, Robert asked everyone who had been on Retreat to stay and meet with him. Robert wanted to cheer us up but not everyone could be cheered. That was the last time I saw Sara and Norma in class—they left and never came back.

Robert came to the next class too and asked to meet the Retreat group afterward again. He'd just learned—apparently from Hazel— that when we had met at Jimmy's apartment we had all discussed leaving. He was furious. "You were plotting a coup!" Robert barked. One by one he made us confess to the accusation. Some of us said that we had been "asleep," but Robert would have none of that "Work-talk." He said, "This is not sleep, it's violence and pure evil. For everything School and Sharon do for you, all you can do is to think about how to kill her and kill School? If you think you can leave and still have the power of the Work, you are sadly mistaken. You will lose your connection to consciousness if you leave. You will lose it all. You all make me sick. I could puke."

I tried to talk to Beth when we got home. But she was mentally and physically worn out. She had given one of the most tearful allocutions of guilt during the Robert meeting, agreeing that she had been "treasonous." Ultimately, Beth didn't want to leave. Her connection was too deep. She cried to me, "I've been with Sharon so long in School. If I left it would be like admitting I wasted my whole life on a fraud." I said that we were "throwing good money after bad" by staying. But she was adamant. She wanted to stay. I agreed. We had a son. I wanted to keep our family together. I didn't want to leave without her, because that would have ended our marriage. After that night, Beth and I never discussed the subject of leaving School.

Back to "Normal"

In *One Flew Over the Cuckoo's Nest,* there is a scene where McMurphy returns to the ward after his frontal lobotomy. The chaos, the uprising, the violence, and the suicide are ancient history, wiped clean. Order is restored. The music is once again monotonously serene. Everything is back to normal.

After all our tumult, School also went back to normal. Order was restored. Rules (like no fraternization) which had been relaxed were now reinstated. We now read out loud during class the self-observations we wrote in our daily journals so that teachers could hear what we were thinking and feeling during private moments. We were asked to start saying a morning prayer whereby one asks immediately upon awakening, "God, what can I do for you today?" and to wait for an answer. We would also read these out in class. Sharon promoted those of us from Retreat who stayed to become leaders of study groups we held during class. She even promoted some to teachers: both Kim and Beth were now full-fledged teachers. It was the ultimate honor. This lifted Beth's morale. Beth was now my teacher. Some of us were made "sustainers," which meant that we were each assigned three new students. As sustainers we were to hand in weekly reports about our conversations with our charges. That's when I realized how Sharon knew so much about me in the early years. Sustainers were spies. I asked to be relieved as a sustainer. I also asked to be relieved as a study group leader.

But I was resigned to my fate—I was in School for better or worse. I decided to make the best of it, including trying harder to do all the exercises and practice the Work ideas. I also tried to build new friendships with other men in class. I hoped that without all the unrest, School would get better—only the more serious students were left; I secretly hoped that Sharon would retire and disband School.

The only reason that class was cancelled on September 11, 2001, was that the Space was less than a mile from Ground Zero and the area was locked down. But we met two nights later in a meeting space in the Barbizon Hotel. Fred rose to the occasion and helped soothe us. Yes, Fred had come back from the wilderness. No explanation was given about why he returned: he just showed up one night without fanfare or announcement as though he had never left. But Fred was different—calmer and less prone to tantrums. He didn't get involved with personal matters during class, those issues were addressed by Sharon. Sharon had calmed down too, if only for a while.

The next crisis came in early 2002, when Lianne's documentary, *Artists and Orphans: A True Drama* was nominated for an Academy Award for Best Documentary. Somehow, she had gotten Rosie O'Donnell, a champion for children, to agree to do the narration for the film. Sharon was overjoyed. She was the star and attended all the run-up parties in LA. It was the happiest I'd seen her. But it wouldn't be for long. Somehow, Rosie learned that Lianne was part of a "cult" that was homophobic and racist. Rosie demanded, during her hugely popular daytime television talk show, that her voice be removed from the film. There was a lot of bad press. We were cautioned not to read it—they were "lies and poisonous." I disobeyed. I found a website, culteducation.com., run by someone named Rick Alan Ross, a leading cult expert. He posted an essay written by former School members. I had mixed feelings. While the essay contained accurate facts, I didn't think School was a cult. But this part caught my eye. It was all new information:

Teachers at the Gans schools never discuss the history of the group, and students who ask are often intimidated into never asking again. What is known is that Alex Horn established a group in northern California with his wife. Interestingly, one of Alex Horn's early students was supposedly Robert Burton, who later created the "Fellowship of Friends," a group, which has often been called a "cult" and has a sordid history of sex scandals, bad press, and lawsuits.

Alex Horn later left his wife and established a new group with his new wife Sharon Gans in San Francisco. Sharon Gans is a one-time actress who was featured in the film "Slaughterhouse Five." Sharon and Alex called their new group "The Theatre of All Possibilities" and "Everyman Inc." They held classes, recruited heavily, and used the group as a vehicle for producing Alex Horn's plays, which often starred Ms. Gans.

The new group proved to be a lucrative moneymaker for the Horns. Members provided free labor and were convinced that to do so was a privilege. The Horns' students worked on productions, acted in them, sold tickets on the streets, built sets, prepared and served dinners and provided whatever they could. According to some members whose allegations were later quoted in the press, Alex Horn abused his students both physically and verbally. And Sharon Gans-Horn was known to berate members to keep them in line.

The Horns controlled a substantial income from their students, which was often in cash. But after the *San Francisco Chronicle* ran a story exposing the group in 1978, they seemed to disappear from the Bay area virtually overnight. Sharon and Alex left California and apparently stayed at their ranch in Montana.

Eventually the group once again formed in New York City, except for one prominent follower, Robert, who started a satellite school in Boston under the direction of Sharon Gans and Alex Horn.

The New York group met regularly in people's homes and eventually began renting a meeting space on Broadway in lower Manhattan. Students were also invited to participate in

Retreats at the Falls Creek Ranch in Condon, Montana where there was more intensive instruction and numerous construction projects.

About 1986 a second group was formed in New York and recruiting efforts were stepped up. Alex Horn's behavior was a problem though and during the late 80s he was effectively removed as the group's leader through a kind of coup. By the end of 1988 Sharon Gans had sole control of the organization both in New York and Boston. Though Alex Horn retained a handful of students in Manhattan, Sharon Gans remains in control to this day.

Members refer to the Gans led group as "The Work" or simply "school." The group has recently incorporated under the name of "Odyssey Study Group." Ms. Gans and/or her students have operated under many names, which also include "Good Omen Inc.," "Everyman Inc.," "Davail Inc.," "Fountain Ridge," "New York Playwrights Association" and "Falls Creek Ranch."

It all had the ring of truth, but I suspected—as Sharon said—that the former students had an ax to grind, were disgruntled, and they could not be trusted. But I couldn't un-remember what I read, and the seeds of my unraveling involvement in School were planted. For Sharon, however, the Academy Award/Rosie debacle tipped a scale for her and she got crazier and sicker and more wicked.

Sharon Nights, Part IV: The Sharon Show

She was the actress who couldn't land a gig. Too difficult to work with. Too eccentric. Too untalented. So she started her own show: "The Sharon Show" a.k.a. The Work. She was now, in the waning days, coming twice weekly to "star" in Manhattan and sometimes in Boston. With general admission ranging from $300 to $500 per month she was still pulling in quite a haul from her students. And she wasn't letting them out of her sights. Her audience winnowed to the loyal, desperate, and the hooked; they were imprisoned in her inter-active, immersive show.

Imagine: Sharon likes to keep her audience waiting as they sit silently. The seventy-ish-year-old star and her minions, the four "junior teachers" can be heard laughing and rousing it up for forty-five or so minutes backstage in Sharon's suite. They are dining on caviar, grilled lamb, and drinking Absolut on the rocks. Finally, the audience can hear the suite's door open and the star and her entourage laughing, gabbing, and walking the long hallway that leads to the stage of the classroom. The house lights are dimmed, and the sound system blares the solo trumpet from Copland's "Fanfare for the Common Man."

We jump to our feet. We are arranged on four rows of seats on risers facing the front of the room. Our eyes betray anxiety, dread, and mild panic; but we pretend to be delighted to see the star. As she enters from the back of the room, the spotlight is on her and she and walks up the center aisle which separates the risers. "Hello Sharon," we cheer. There she is! Live, in person. The foot-high pile of bright orange hair. The deeply set cerulean eyes. The pale skin. The gaudy gold earrings and diamond rings. Sometimes she wears her Bulgari sunglasses at night. She wears her trademark long dress, fit for a medieval queen. She shuffles down the aisle waving to her fans, occasionally making small talk and greeting some individually, like the president. Then, two of her minions hurry her along and lift her by her arms to the wooden platform where sits her leather La-Z-Boy and a side table with finger foods, a water glass, her Absolut on the rocks in a stem glass, and a small vase with a single rose of Sharon. She shoos away her helpers as if to show her own resilience and then plops herself down for her performance. Seemingly summoning all her strength, she reaches her right hand down to yank back the La-Z-Boy lever. In the second between that yank and the extension of the La-Z-Boy, we take our seats and experience growling stomachs, racing hearts, jumbled minds, sweaty palms, twitchy eyes, the jitters. That's because when that La-Z-Boy extends and Sharon is laid back and comfy, the show begins and one of us will be chosen at random to participate in the show—one where someone volunteers for a magic trick that always goes awry and terribly maims the volunteer. Sharon has been doing this show since the 1970s; she could do it backward, in her sleep, and you never know how she will open it until she selects the first person. Tonight, it's going to be one of her favorite scenes: *Public Humiliation of Select Audience Members*. The silent prayers, "Please God not that one, please God not me, not me."

The La-Z-Boy extends. She begins. She is a master. She looks straight out scanning the room for her first victim to bully and humiliate. She has learned, however, to read her crowd well, and tonight she reads unease. So, to warm them up, she does a head fake and opens up with another scene: *These Are a Few of My Favorite Toadies*. And her toady of the moment (she tends to recycle her bootlickers) is Phil, in the front row. Phil is by most estimations gay and agreed to Sharon's version of conversion therapy—she makes arranged marriages of gay men to straight women. Phil was set up with Karen, a recently wid-owed woman (whom Sharon had viciously blamed for the accidental death of her first husband).

Sharon is cranky tonight, you can tell. We are scared and uneasy. But her expression of contempt and disgust for the audience changes to a slight smile when she gives Phil the nod, which is her cue for him to speak. Phil beams and starts, "Thank you Sharon, it is so wonderful to see you. I feel so privileged to have the great good fortune of being your student. I have an affirmation to share with you and the class." With pride he boasts, "Last weekend we visited Karen's father—an evil being—and I stood up for myself as a man for my wife." Sharon's slight smile turns to a full smile, her eyes widen, and she loudly sings in her falsetto, "Oh Phil, how wonderful." She claps and the audience gives a standing ovation. We are all very relieved by her brightened mood. But we are simultaneously repulsed by Phil and the favored treatment he receives from our teacher, whom we all rely upon for our own self-worth and validation. Basing one's happiness on a wildly volatile, arbitrary, and deranged leader is a dangerous business—most of us are miserable. But we are hooked on confirmation from Sharon.

So, back to poor Phil living a completely manufactured existence. What was his affirmation all about? What he did, at Sharon's request, was to *demand that Karen's evil father (a rather wealthy fellow) give money to Karen and Phil for their new family*. Having wealthy family members give money to her followers is a favorite pastime of Sharon; it gets her really hot and really horny. So she was really turned on by this good news. That is because a lot of the money ends up in her pockets—a tithing. What a relief for the audience. But soon she had her eyes out for someone else.

Hazel thinks the coast is clear. Poor silly Hazel. She's betting that Sharon is now in a good mood anticipating that windfall from Kar-en's father and will give her some positive reinforcement. So, she seizes the opportunity. She leaps to her feet so violently that the riser shakes and almost buckles. She is almost out of breath with excite-ment as she shares her epiphany. "Thank you, Sharon. It is wonderful to be here—I am so fortunate. I want to share with you that I am really now finally beginning to really see what a liar I am."

The entire audience quickly looks to gauge Sharon's reaction. Uh, oh. No good. Cringe time. We've seen this scene play out the same way *every fucking time*. All breathing in the room stops. We are about to witness Hazel receive a new orifice. Our seats creak with our shifting weights. The room is still. This is the exact moment Sharon most relishes—when she can brutalize her most loyal minion—even her Uriah Heep—just because she feels like it. Like a predator, Sharon pounces. She shakes her head in disgust, looks downward at her long fingernails, and snorts in contempt, "Hazel, you don't have the slightest idea of what a *hateful, repugnant,* and *pathological* liar you really are. Why the hell are you standing? Why? Sit down. Yes, sit down." Hazel sits down, chastened, and sheepishly nods to Sharon. We hear not a peep from Hazel for the rest of the evening. (Later, after class, I approach Hazel to gauge how she's doing and she assures me that Sharon gave her "gold.") Indeed, Sharon has been calling Hazel a liar for many decades, projecting onto her. Hazel makes this kind of false confession every six months or so. It never works to assuage Sharon or to get her approval. It only escalates the public humiliations, making matters worse. Over the years we have seen Hazel demeaned to the point of hyperventilating and wetting herself.

Why does Hazel keep coming back for more? Because she craves Sharon's attention like she craves the air to breathe. It's an existential need. Abuse is the only attention Hazel gets from Sharon, so she takes it. Like a child clinging to a violent parent. The audience painfully recognizes and understands this but not a single person challenges Sharon or comes to Hazel's aid. Because—teachers, older students, younger students, everyone—we're all in the same boat as Hazel. We cannot do enough for Sharon.

Back to the show: After eviscerating Hazel, the blood drips from Sharon's mouth. And she wants more. But nobody wants to get up to speak. Usually, one toady or another can be counted upon to speak. But they aren't foolish enough to jump in tonight. Only Danny is. He stands and states, "Sharon, I need to bring back some work." Danny is a loose cannon. Brace yourselves. This is going to be a bumpy night.

Danny is perpetually oblivious to this topsy-turvy-make-believe-Gans-world—and loves to speak in class at any opportunity. He is unliked by most students because he has learned to emulate the leaders and is abusive to others. Like Phil, Danny is also a gay man who was married off by Sharon to a woman in class. His wife was a single mother named Paula. Understandably, they have an unhappy marriage. We all wince. What will it be this time from Danny: a graphic sexual grievance about his wife and how he'd like to cheat on her (while she is sitting right next to him), something about his childhood where he was mistreated by his parents (something which Sharon belittles), or even problems in his job (common for him)?

But Sharon is one step ahead. She ignores Danny's question and zeroes in on Paula. Her voice filled with contempt, she sneers at Paula, "What is your problem?" Paula jumps to her feet asking, "Me?" "Yes, you," returns Sharon, who continues, "Why won't you be a good wife and screw your husband and take care of him?" Paula is under the klieg lights and responds, "My husband isn't attracted to me." Sharon lets out a bloodcurdling scream. "That's because you're a bad wife. He's a good man. I mean, he was good enough to marry you." Paula is silent, staring straight ahead. We are so glad we aren't her. But no one stands to her defense; not even her husband. Sharon harangues Paula for a good fifteen minutes. Sharon even goes so low as to blame Paula for the accidental death of her younger brother, an event that traumatized Paula.

Sharon's approach to trauma is like Nancy Reagan's direction to kids to "Just say no" to drugs. Sharon tells those with traumas to "Just get over it." For example, Lori needs to just get over the time when she was a nine-year-old girl and found her mother hanging in the kitchen: "You cannot get on with your life if you don't just get over it. Just get over it." Rhonda needs to just get over that time she was raped and almost murdered in her home by an intruder: "You need to go to this man and apologize to him because your negative vibrations actually caused him to attack you. Just get over it." Alan needs to just get over walking in on his wife sleeping with his best friend—"If you had been a good husband, she wouldn't have been fucking him." Just get over it.

After class, I drive Sharon Gans home.

PART 5
2010–January 2013

Happy Birthday

I'd had my foot out the door for almost a decade, ever since Jimmy, Seth, Peter, and the others left. But I'd been shackled by an arranged marriage to Beth and one of my biggest clients, the real estate tycoon Andre Podonok. I hadn't planned on even going to class the night of my birthday. In the early days, classes were time well spent, but now they were a forced march and a colossal waste of my time. I knew this would be a typical night: A teacher would be lecturing for the hundredth time to fifty sleep-deprived, bored Manhattan professionals on Gurdjieff's enchantingly dreary *Beelzebub's Tales to His Grandson: An Objectively Impartial Criticism of the Life of Man*. But a student named Carmella had called to ask me to come.

I went and at some point Fred shuffled into the room balancing a white coconut cake with five lit candles (each representing a decade of my life) while the entire class sang a rousing version of you know what. Even before I blew out the candles, I felt the smoke being blown up my ass. I'd been flattered, sweet-talked, groomed, and abused by Sharon, Fred, Robert, and the other so-called teachers, and the blinders were off. But I also believed I owed them everything and I feared them, and I desperately needed them. I blew out the candles and endured thirty minutes of toasts by my classmates, such as "Spencer, I have seen you grow from an angry twenty-nine-year-old to a real man of the Work with a rich life" or "I love you and your unique perspective and courage" or "You are on the verge of a break-through." Blah, blah, blah.

Then Fred raised his glass of champagne and gave the final toast to my "keen mind" and his fervent wish that I "transform" my "impetuous and surly and insolent personality," at which point Felix jumped up and said to Fred, "What kind of toast is this? It's his birth-day." The classroom erupted and everyone piled on Felix. "Fuck you, Felix." "How dare you speak like that to Fred?" And my brain hit a switch and the Work entered me like an IV drip and even I jumped in to defend Fred, saying he was giving me a "blessing"—a gift. And I thanked the Work and my friends and my teachers, and I meant it, even as I knew I was locking myself up in an even more secure cell. I couldn't help it.

My Second Story[28]

Our thirteen-year marriage was unraveling. It had been for a while. There was no real foundation. We'd married quickly. Under pressure. We never recovered after the exodus of our friends many summers before. Beth's decision to stay showed me that School was more important to her than I was. And she knew I knew that. Beth had put our marriage second to School. And Sharon's promotion of Beth to teacher status had placed me as second to Beth. Sharon was an untenable third party in our marriage, making any problem, any issue, a matter for public consumption.

My belief and hope that passion and intimacy would grow in our marriage was a mirage. Beth and I were unhappy, regretful, bitter, and lonely. We were suffering. But despite all that, I viewed divorce as a personal failure and shortcoming, as well as a disappointment to Sharon. I preferred to be in a loveless, sexless marriage than not in one at all.

Sharon suggested that Beth and I start to see a marriage counselor for therapy. She recommended Dr. Frank White who had an office

---

28 According to School, everyone's life is a "Three Story House." The "First Story" is work or money; the "Second Story" is sex or family; the "Third Story" is aspiration or religion. Sharon said it was necessary to develop each story.

on West Thirteenth Street in the Village. Dr. White saw us weekly for a few months.

Dr. White didn't seem to be experienced in marriage counseling: he provoked arguments and let them play out. We came out of sessions feeling worse than when we'd entered, and we suspected he and Sharon were talking about us. One time he blurted out to Beth, "Did it ever occur to you that maybe the reason your husband and you don't have sex anymore is because he is a homosexual?" Beth was caught off guard and said no. Dr. White looked at me knowingly, and asked, "How about you, do you think you are a homosexual?" There was nothing in our sessions that could have possibly made him think this. Did Sharon discuss this with him? Did she tell him I "experimented" with my camp counselor? I told Dr. White exactly what had happened to me: that a twenty-year-old man made me touch him when I was fourteen. But I said I was not gay, had no attraction toward men, and yet that this event had left some doubts in my mind about my sexuality.

Dr. White listened carefully, his expression revealing his apparent belief that he had indeed "gotten somewhere." He looked at us both, took some notes, and said, "Well I think your sexual preference is an issue we can discuss separately" at another time.

Shortly after this session, on a random weekday night in 2009, Beth and I stood in our tiny New York City apartment kitchen. Our backs to each other, she opened the fridge to put away the skim milk, and I was at the sink washing the dishes. Without any prelude, she said, "Oh, I hired a divorce lawyer today. Where do you want him to serve the papers on you?" This was so abrupt and casual: the first time the D word had come up. I smelled a rat, one with red hair. I turned to face her, but she was already walking into the living room to sit at her desk, facing away. "What? Are you joking?" I said. Looking down at her paperwork she said, "I'll tell him to serve you at the office."

Early the next morning, my office phone rang. I was expecting her. As usual, Sharon skipped hello: "Spencer, you need to quickly work out the details of your divorce amicably." I responded obsequiously, "Yes, Sharon, I agree. Beth has hired a lawyer already." Annoyed because Beth had apparently disobeyed her instructions to work it out without lawyers, Sharon crowed, "That's ridiculous. No. You two need to work it out without lawyers. Call Beth now and tell her I want you to both come over to my house this afternoon and we can get all the terms resolved in half an hour."

Danger Will Robinson! For twenty years, I reflexively did almost anything Sharon told me to do. No command was too big to ignore: my work life, who I married, what my thoughts should be, where I should live, my very feelings about myself. But this crossed my Maginot Line.

So, at 9:05 a.m., while sitting in my office on the phone with Sharon, staring out of the window at the courthouses with the weary litigants queued up to enter these sausage factories, I did something else. I calculated. Like a computer. All the hundreds of facts in my brain, my memory, and my consciousness were instantly called up, categorized, sorted, and weighed. Divorce would impact my finances in terms of child support and division of assets. It would involve deciding custody issues. And it would profoundly alter my very day-to-day life. Sharon would side with Beth as she always did, it was clear. I couldn't have Sharon deciding anything or having a hand in it. If I refused to cooperate, I risked getting kicked out of School. Sharon's ideas of family matters were warped and in divorces she would counsel extreme positions based upon the spouse she liked the best: full custody to one spouse; limited visitation; the house, the cars, the savings to her favored spouse. People would usually comply.[29] My calculation was done in a split second.

I knew that Sharon wanted an out-of-court settlement because she didn't want to be subpoenaed as a witness and to testify. She did

---

29 Sharon's own custody fight went all the way up to the United States Supreme Court, and the case is taught in law schools, a case called *Kulko v. Superior Court of California*, 436 U.S. 84 (1978). There Justice Thurgood Marshall ruled that Sharon's attempt to sue her California-based ex-husband (Ezra Kulko) in New York for child support was a violation of Ezra's due process rights under the United States Constitution. The opinion noted that despite their divorce agreement, Sharon had later convinced her then-teenage children to leave Ezra and move in with her. As a result, her children became estranged from Ezra, although her son reestablished relations with Ezra when he was an adult.

not want to be questioned about School and what she did to people. She knew I would subpoena her too. I said, "Thank you, Sharon. Can you tell me what kind of settlement you would suggest?" She described a one-sided scenario of which no judge would approve, no parent would ever agree, and no child would be able to survive. Having seen Sharon's sick mind operate like this with so many other students, I was ready for something like this—but it was the first time she ever tried to impose something so wretched on me. So I countered, "Sharon, with all due respect, I cannot agree with that. It's not fair and it's also not legal. No judge would ever go along with something like that." She fell silent. I told her what I wanted and what was fair. She volleyed back, but her position was weak. Over the next couple of months, Beth and I finalized the terms (without any input from Sharon), putting the best interests of our son first. But Sharon's deplorable interference in this aspect of my life—and my son's—further cracked my faith in her. Of the final three straws, this was the first.

Now I was a single man at the age of fifty, free from the crushing isolation and loneliness of a School marriage. Couples in arranged School marriages usually have nothing in common except for School. They are married to School with Sharon as a third party, like a throuple. I continued to regularly attend class, but often showed up late. I had no intention to leave School: my biggest client was in School and I couldn't afford to lose him.

The divorce unshackled me from my insulated marriage—Beth did not like to socialize with any of my old friends or family. The first thing I did was to reconnect with them. I began to spend weekends with Joel in Brooklyn and I would go the east end of Long Island with my old friend Colin and his family. I also rekindled my relationship with Matthew and my mother. They treated me as if I hadn't been absent all those years.

Colin reintroduced me to one of my old loves: swimming. One summer morning in 2010, Colin drove us to the East Hampton YMCA lap pool to work out—we'd been on the swim team together in high school. I hadn't swum in years. The pool there is twenty-five yards, has six lanes, and is in a first-floor space with a soaring ceiling and a strip of glass skylights running its length; one wall is glass. That wall faces east, and the sun casts its rays in the pool on clear days, giving the sense of being outside. We changed into our suits in the cramped men's locker room. Colin removed his shirt, and he still had the same fit body from when we were on the swim team. Me, I was a good thirty pounds overweight. Colin and I walked onto the pool deck. He explained that he had a very specific ritual that he encouraged me to follow. He said, "It's all about consistency: keeping pace and coming back to the pool on a regular basis." He swam exactly one mile—no more, no less—seventy-two laps. He would stop after the first thirty-six laps for exactly one minute—no more, no less. I adopted this OCD workout as mine and continued it three times a week, in New York and on Long Island, where I bought a small weekend place. I still went to class twice a week. Other than Podonok, I didn't see or speak to anyone from School outside class, and that was fine with me.

On Thanksgiving Day morning in 2012 at about 7:00 a.m., I jumped into the warm chlorinated basement pool at the YMCA on West Fourteenth Street. The humid air was about ninety-five degrees and water was kept at eighty-two. I had the middle lane all to myself and I felt strong and fast—my arms cutting through and pulling the cloudy turquoise water under my torso, the whooshing of bubbles and my heart gaining in speed. The pain in my life deadened by the endorphins. Two men about my age asked to share the lane. Friendly, they said they had a workout and they cajoled me to join them. Chet had a chiseled swimmer's body, swam on his college team, went to cooking school in France, became a corporate lawyer at a big NYC firm, and played harpsichord. He was divorced. Andrew was from Tulsa, was a big shot at an ad agency, walked around the city taking black-and-white photos, and was also divorced. Their workout consisted of swimming forty-eight laps of butterfly, which I could not possibly do, and I told them that I'd rather go through my divorce again than do their workout. They cracked up. That's when they proffered an invitation to join their Masters swim team, which met every weekday morning at 7:00 a.m. for ninety minutes. I slogged through ten minutes of butterfly and took my leave. There had been no judgment of my performance. I joined the Masters team the next week. There were twenty swimmers on the coed team ranging from their late twenties to their seventies. Andrew and Chet were in the fast lane, but I had to start out in the slow lane, which was fine. I was in that lane with Erma, a pregnant investment banker from China; Maryann, an artist from the Village; Sharona, a midwife who also did stand-up comedy; Francis, a dentist and forensic scientist and rapper; and Frank, a barrel-chested accountant from Illinois. They welcomed me with good spirit. Within a couple of weeks I was moved to the faster lane. The workouts were challenging, and it wasn't easy for me—especially with being in class until 2:00 a.m. So I scheduled my swims accordingly and I started to show up for class less. Sometimes, after workouts, I joined my fellow swimmers for coffee before heading to work.

My First Story

By 2012, I was working almost full-time for Podonok: his business had grown, and we relied on each other. I still had my own office uptown and other clients, but now he was one of the biggest. The dynamics changed. He made extraordinary demands on my time, wanted me to handle personal matters for him, was getting slow in paying me, and started to use Work ideas, guilt, and his connection with Sharon to manipulate me. He thought he owned me. He did. "Where the hell are you?" he barked at me once when he couldn't get me on the phone immediately because I was downstairs getting a sandwich. "You don't go out for lunch when you're working on my matters." He called me at home one evening, demanding I come back into my office, screaming at me, "You don't leave your office until I tell you—where is your Aim?" Podonok was shrewd and knew how to handle people, especially when he felt he had the upper hand. He knew that I was highly dependent upon him for my income. I was a kept man.

One afternoon, I got a call: "Hello, this is William Ruckus of the New York State Attorney General's Office. Is this Spencer Schneider?" He explained that the AG was going to be coming to examine the Podonok Company business records. He hung up and I tried to gather my wits. This was unusual. When I received their email moments later asking for documents, I saw the problem: it was School.

Former students who hated Podonok called the AG claiming (falsely) that he was a front for Sharon, and they decided to investigate.

A couple of weeks later, in early August 2012, Ruckus and two other AG examiners holed up in Podonok's conference room to examine thousands of pages of documents and asked for more information on a daily basis.

I didn't know what they would find. I was worried. I was Podonok's counsel, and concerned that they might try to hold me responsible for anything that they might dig up on him. Moreover, Podonok and his staff were slow to provide documents. More troubling, however, Podonok was highly secretive with me about his dealings with Sharon, raising suspicions in my mind. And he was dismissive of the investigation, didn't take it seriously, and even joked at one point that he should try to hire one of the investigators. "She would be jumping for joy working for me," he quipped.

One day, the AG examiners and their supervisor called Podonok and me into the conference room, shut the door, and cross-examined us about School. They wanted to know about Sharon, what School was like, whether it was hierarchical, why it was secretive, what we studied, and several other questions having nothing to do whatsoever with anything. It seemed intrusive, unnecessary, and designed to harass us. But it had a terrible effect on me: it got me even more paranoid and anxious than I already was, thinking that they were on to something about something and that I had done something and that they were going to hold this something against me. I didn't come to class for about a month: I was afraid the AG or the FBI was following me and tapping my phones. I had images of them going through my trash.

Luckily, however, the meeting was the last time they asked about School or Podonok's involvement with School. It now became clearer, however, that the AG was no longer interested in School but was now questioning other aspects of Podonok's business. Podonok insisted that he had not done anything wrong, and he wanted to fight. But I was concerned that the government's resources were unlimited and that he could avoid the huge expense and distraction of a fight by paying some nominal amount without admitting he'd done anything wrong and moving on. A proud man, he considered that option to be defeat and viewed my position as a betrayal. Podonok had a binary view: either you were loyal to him, or you were not. I'd crossed his line and now I was in danger. He was capable of anything and might even try to scapegoat me with the AG.

I became so anxious I could barely eat. When I could sleep I was having nightmares. So I decided to call Sharon. Podonok and I frequently consulted with Sharon concerning our business together and she'd gladly offered advice throughout the years. She also successfully mediated a couple of times when Podonok and I had disagreements.

It was a weekday afternoon in October 2012 at around 3:00 p.m. in a crowded pedestrian-only plaza, filled with tourists getting in the way of harried New Yorkers. I hadn't eaten all day. I was weak. I was mentally spent. Emotionally tattered. I was frightened and I was desperate. It was a clear day and the buildings cast sharp shadows on the frenetic plaza. The sweet smell of roasting sugar peanuts made my stomach growl and I looked over to see the vendor filling up his small waxy bags with the hot nuts. I dialed Sharon. She answered almost immediately. I explained to her in detail what was going on with the AG and Podonok and the risks involved. "Sharon, please speak some sense into Andre and suggest he take care of this before it blows up in his face." My cell phone was pressed up hard against my ear. I strained to hear and then Sharon yelled, "I don't give a flying fuck about the AG, they can go and fuck themselves. This has nothing to do with me and I don't give a shit." At that moment, I thought, *You don't give a shit about me. You don't care about the risks I face? It would mean nothing, take nothing for you to speak with Podonok. He would listen to you. I've given you my life.* This was the penultimate straw.

The next morning, walking across West Fourteenth Street on the way to the subway from the pool, I was obsessing about Podonok. He was no longer listening to me, and I believed he was headed to a risky, expensive, and senseless battle with the AG. I also knew that

he emulated and was entirely devoted to Sharon. I felt Podonok getting into a fight with the AG was a perfect storm of stubbornness,
naiveté, and hubris. Plus he was now holding back payments from
me out of spite (and I surmised) with Sharon's blessing. I hadn't
eaten in twenty-four hours. I was losing four pounds a week. I had
to escape his orbit and I started to plan my escape from him and try
to rebuild a law practice. But for some period—and I didn't know
how long—I would have very little income, or business. I had to
plan for the worst case, calculating how much I had in the bank to
cover my rent, my child support payments to Beth, my mortgage,
and all my other expenses. I figured I had about twelve months
before I'd be broke. I didn't think I could possibly remake myself
within a year.

And then those thoughts came up. Those thoughts I'd had for
many years now—I guess I could just end my life. I thought of poor
Hiram Cosby and Kenny and how they got relief by taking their lives.
This option became appealing, and I became obsessed with this. The
thoughts filled my days. And there was nobody to turn to.

I called Matthew, telling him that I was having more suicidal
thoughts than I normally did. "Normally do? Spencer, it's not normal
to *ever* have these thoughts." He gave me the number of a psychiatrist
who was a friend of a friend.[30]

A few days later I found myself sitting in a worn upholstered
armchair facing Dr. Light. We were alone in a small room. He had no
receptionist, just a waiting room with a side table and copies of the
New Yorker and Psychology Today. Dr. Light had sympathetic brown eyes
and a gentle handshake. He spoke slowly and called me Mr. Schneider.
The sun poured in from the single window behind me, warming the
back of my neck. I smelled what I thought was sandalwood incense.
A small bronze Buddha sat on the side table to my right behind the
box of tissues. I came here to talk about my dark thoughts about
ending my life and to a lesser degree the fears I was having about the
AG investigation. But I hadn't planned on telling him anything about

---

30   If you are having thoughts of suicide, please put down this book and call the
     National Suicide Prevention Lifeline by dialing 988.

School. He asked how he could help. "I came to see you because I'm going crazy," I told him.

After determining that I wasn't having any visual or audio hallucinations or delusions, he assured me that I was not crazy.

I just sat there and looked at him. I thought he was trying to be clever and cheer me up. I said, "Dr. Light, I'm not crazy in the sense that I'm hearing voices or think the government is controlling my mind, but I truly feel like I'm going crazy."

Dr. Light did not react but pressed his point, saying I didn't have any indications of serious psychological disorders. He said, "I understand that there are things that are troubling you and we can talk about whatever you want, but you are not crazy or going crazy—there is just no evidence of that, I'm sorry." I relented. Dr. Light was playing the rationality card. I would let it go for now. But it was making me feel a lot better.

I spoke to Kim by phone a few days later, hoping to convince her to convey the seriousness of my situation to Sharon. She said that I had to stop having "negative imagination." She said I was not working hard enough on myself.

The Last Impression

The 2012 Christmas Class was a dismal affair. It took place at a dilapidated church on West Fifty-Seventh Street that apparently did not have much of a congregation anymore. They rented the chapel to us for $300 for twenty-four hours. I believe it could have been used as either a set for *Young Frankenstein* or a car garage. The place smelled of horse manure from a nearby stable.

Although I had no intention of leaving School, my heart wasn't in it anymore, and for this I felt guilty and wretched. I didn't participate at all in the preparations and was even considering not going, which was the equivalent of declaring war personally on Sharon and would have made my miserable life more miserable. So I went. But it was surreal just showing up without having had any kind of involvement—like walking into a test without having done any homework. I felt distant. It was obvious that my connection with School was unraveling. I had seen it happen many times with other students: you can tell when the love is gone. The faraway look, the sadness, the spell broken.

The low point of the evening came during Sharon's remarks following a cold and tasteless dinner. This was the traditional speech where Sharon either thanks the class for the evening and speaks about the Christmas season, consciousness, and brotherly love, or something random ticks her off and she attacks us. Sharon spotted Karen, who was recently pregnant with twins, and said, "Congratulations Karen, you look wonderful." The entire class oohed and ahhed. And then Joni spoke up and said, "And congratulations to you too, Peter." Joni was about sixty-seven, a diabetic, and was recovering from her second heart attack. A lovely woman, she had been in School for decades. But her remark fell like a thud. We instinctively knew that Joni had crossed the line and had made a serious gaffe. Half of the people in attendance didn't know that Karen and Peter were married because they attended the other class during the week. Sharon, who regulated information such as this, had never informed the other class for reasons known only to her. But the point was that it was Sharon's sole prerogative to share this information between the classes and she hated anyone stealing her lines, as it were. Sharon came down on Joni, but gently, saying, "Well Joni, thank you, but we are talking to Karen tonight only." The night ended without further incident.

I had been coming to classes for twenty-three years and I had witnessed every scene countless times. But now the anesthesia of School was slowly wearing off. I felt the cold steel of the grinding drill penetrating the rotten tooth, just a hair away from the exposed nerve. Every muscle in my body was tensed and the dentist's assistant was holding me down in the chair. The annual post-Christmas class— called the Impressions Class (so named because we each relayed our "impressions" of what a great evening it was) was held a week later, in late December 2012.

Sharon hobbled into class, and we could see she was unhappy. She said nothing. She was helped in by Fred and Beth. She plopped herself down, wincing in pain, and shut her eyes. When she opened them she stared at Joni and roared at the top of her lungs: "You've got a big mouth. How dare you open your trap. It's none of your business to thank anyone. You are asleep. Asleep! It is killing me, and you are trying to kill School too."

It took a minute for me to even remember what Joni's infraction had been. For her part, Joni was ashen, standing, trembling, quiet, and it occurred to me that she might not survive this attack. It went on for fifteen minutes while Sharon lay flat on her leather La-Z-Boy. Fred sitting by her side looked concerned for Sharon's condition. All other eyes were fixed on Joni. Nobody (not even Joni) had any pity for Joni. But the drill was coming close to my root, and I felt the steel of hate and violence. The class had devolved into automatons, robots—lifeless sycophants. Nobody spoke up—including me—and I was ashamed of myself.

No amount of Joni's apologies satisfied Sharon's wrath. It only made matters worse.

Then—in a scene reminiscent of that time in Georgia with Natia—Sharon started to cry, claiming that Joni's actions were a personal attack on Sharon, herself. This led to an outpouring of sympathy for Sharon, and the class railed against Joni, shouting at her for being "asleep." Joni was about to faint, so she sat down and started to heave. The outrage against her only intensified. Some people demanded that she "stand up" and take the "help" she was getting. I was afraid for her life.

Next several of the other "teachers"—the capos—including Kim and Maude—mercilessly berated Joni and lashed out at her for her cowardice. Hazel was particularly brutal as she delighted in proving her loyalty to Sharon.

This sickening sight. This horror show. I couldn't tolerate it. And I couldn't hide it anymore. Sharon fixed her gaze on me. I was in the first row of the room. I braced myself. She bellowed, "Stop being negative." I said, *"Me?"* "Yeah you!" She shook her head. And that was the last straw.

When class ended, I left, and, although I didn't know it then, that was the last time I would ever see Sharon or any of my classmates.

New York University's Elmer Bobst Library is a twelve-story rust-colored stone box standing on the southeast corner of Washington Square Park. In 2010, a pair of red-tailed hawks built a nest on a twelfth-floor window ledge of the building. It is a federal crime to disturb a raptor's nest, and so it stayed there. NYU allowed the *New York Times* to install a webcam to broadcast the comings and goings of the nascent family. At my wits end, in 2012, I spent hours, daily, watching this webcam. Hooked. During work, at home over dinner, when I woke up, when I got up in the middle of night to go to the bathroom.

The nest consisted of branches, twigs, leaves, and paper litter. The rusty walls and floor of the ledge were splattered with bird shit in the manner of Jackson Pollock. Hawk couples mate for life and share parenting duties—egg sitting, hunting, and feeding. The eggs are dull white with black specks. At birth the chicks are covered with white fuzzy down and appear no different than baby chickens, which is why I stopped eating poultry. They are helpless puffs. In the first weeks they spend most of their time under their parent's breasts. The chicks are treated to local, freshly killed squirrels, rabbits, rats, mice, pigeons, and other birds. The hunter will return to the nest with the meal still in its talons and then split the furry skin with its beak until it reaches the bloody meat. It will tear away a small warm morsel and place it down the throat of the chick. This family of hawks, having made its home in the heart of New York City, captivated me. It calmed me.

Kimberly

I met Kimberly on a red-eye from Seattle to JFK. She was a flight attendant and said to me at the door, "Hello, welcome aboard," and it seemed like an original sincere statement, customized for me. In my fragile state, any act of kindness moved me. I didn't distinguish the fact that she was just doing her job. I asked, "Wait, is this the one to JFK?" Apparently, this was the funniest thing she had heard all day, and she placed her hand on my shoulder as if to hold herself up while she laughed, "I hope so."

On an overnight flight, passengers drift in and out of sleep and the flight attendants act like nannies who tend the slumbering. When I wasn't sleeping, I hoped for Kimberly to walk down the aisle. We talked when we could. She gave me a tea bag from her personal stash.

When we landed, I asked for her email address, and she wrote it down on a Delta napkin. I offered to take her to tea when she returned to New York, and she agreed.

A few weeks later we were walking along the Atlantic Ocean on the deserted stretch of beach in a village called Atlantic Beach on Long Island, twenty minutes from where I grew up. We were bundled up in heavy coats for our walk as the weak winter sun set in the west. Kimberly and I talked about our lives, our histories, our plans, our disappointments, our successes, our troubles, our hopes. The beach washed away my inhibitions, and I felt safe with this transient stranger.

Alone with her on this beach, I spoke of the secret I had never told anyone for twenty-three years. I told her about School.

"We study Gurdjieff and his followers," I said, "but the group is very intense and encompasses much more. It's also secret. We aren't allowed to talk about it with anyone, not even family or friends."

"Not even family? Why not?" she asked, growing suspicious, concerned.

"Well, it's meant to be an esoteric school, and by definition we have to keep it hidden."

"Spencer, if you don't mind me saying, that sounds a little off, a little strange to me. Are you sure it's legitimate?" she said.

Suddenly, it didn't sound so legitimate to me either.

Then I told her everything: the tuition, the teachers, the abuse, the total control, Podonok, Joni, and now the closing in of my life.

When I finished, she stopped walking and turned to face me. "Spencer," she said, "I think you might want to reconsider your involvement in this group. I'm concerned for you. I have been involved in abusive situations, and this sounds like one. There is no reason to stay. I know what you're going through."

I had both hoped and been afraid to hear this.

"If I leave the group, I will probably lose my entire business and friends."

She said, "No, Spencer, it's the exact opposite. You don't have anything to lose. It's not a genuine group. They are hurting you."

I looked at her and took a deep breath, tasting the salt, and Kimberly's scent. I thanked her.

My worst fears about School had been confirmed by a third party. Kimberly didn't say much, but what she said had a profound impact on me.

We met again for dinner on my birthday. I completely forgot that it was a class night.

The next morning, on January 10, 2013, I saw that Kim, from School, had left a message on my voice mail at 1:00 a.m., in a frenzied tone: "Spencer, Sharon told me to tell you that it is unacceptable for you not to come to class and that maybe it's time for you to leave School." I called her back.

I said, "Hi, Kim, I got your message."

She asked, "Where were you last night?"

This was a typical question for School, but my response was not typical: "It's really none of your business. I was busy."

This was insolent. This was an answer that meant fuck off. My answer stunned me as much as it did her.

Silence.

"Well," she said, "Sharon thinks maybe it's time for you to leave School because you've been missing so many classes."

I didn't think before I spoke. "I totally agree: maybe it is time for me to leave School."

She interrupted, "No, no, no, no, no, Sharon is not saying you should leave at all. She doesn't want you to leave. This is just a shock to help you get over whatever interval you are crossing now. Sharon wants to shock you," she said in a panicked tone. Her plan was backfiring. Sharon would be furious.

I let her squirm. "Kim, Sharon is absolutely right for me to think about this, and I'm going to follow her instructions and consider whether it's time for me to leave."

I told her I'd get back to her in two weeks, hung up, and took the uptown train to Union Square. I hadn't experienced a sense of power like this in years.

When I got out at Union Square, she called me again. She sounded peppy, energized because (as I expected) she'd just spoken with Sharon, who had a customized message for me. In a solemn tone suggesting she had just conferred with Queen Elizabeth herself, Kim said, "Sharon said that you should come to class on Tuesday and talk about it in front of your friends. This is not something to think about on your own." And then she said something that severed any remaining connection to Sharon and School. Kim said, "Sharon wants you to come into class and get up in front of your friends and be a man."

Be a man? That's exactly what I haven't been: I have been a robot. I said, "Kim, thank you very much, but actually I am a man. Don't contact me anymore." I hung up the phone, and from that moment, was officially out of School.

PART 6
January 2013–Present

It is . . . spiritual freedom—which cannot be taken away—that makes life meaningful and purposeful.

Viktor E. Frankl, *Man's Search for Meaning*

Perfectionism is the belief that something is broken—you.

Edith Eger, *The Choice: Embrace the Possible*

Over and Out

I stopped attending classes, threw out all the Gurdjieff and Ouspensky books, threw out all my self-observation notebooks, stopped saying my Mantra and the morning prayer, stopped working on my five-week Aim, stopped self-sensing and recollecting my day, ceased all communications with anyone in School, and I quit working for Podonok. I was free. I suddenly had two free nights a week. I could do anything. Yet this was a freedom not unlike that of the prisoner who, having served a two-decade sentence for a crime he didn't commit, walks out of the prison gates and is met by no one, has nowhere to go, has nothing but the clothes on his back.

I had virtually no business—at age fifty-three I would have to rebuild from scratch without the support of School, upon which I had relied for decades. My nerves and emotional state were in free fall. I was having nightmares that I was still in School being humiliated and ridiculed by Sharon and my classmates. I was paranoid that the Podonok AG investigation would ensnare me. My thoughts were still School thoughts, centered on the conviction that I alone had caused my misfortune, that my flaws were permanent, and that I didn't have any answers. My "self" had been ground away, snuffed out during the past twenty-three years. My dignity, self-esteem, pride, and self-reliance were distant memories. I was unable to discern reality: I thought that all I had accomplished in my life were gifts from School and that all the troubles Sharon caused me were my fault. Now, I had nothing.

It dawned on me it was going to be harder to get *over* School than it was to get *out*. I didn't have the tools, energy, or the will to do this on my own.

I called Dr. Light to schedule an appointment. I told him it was urgent, and what was going on. He told me to come in the next day.

I sat in Dr. Light's swivel armchair, facing him, ten feet away. There was a couch in his office to the left, which looked no softer than a metal park bench. I was relieved he didn't ask me to lay down. I considered the couch a symbol of failure and intractable mental illness. It meant that one needed decades of professional help. The swivel chair suggested a shorter course of treatment—I was on his eye level. The small Buddha and tissues were on the side table. I didn't think I would need the tissues, but Buddha was calming.

I had been in School for twenty-three years, or 201,480 hours. Therapy was not going to be able to untangle things overnight. It might work that way on television but that's not how it works. Yet there were illuminations, moments of clarity, glimpses, and observations which came up in individual sessions and I rarely left a session without feeling better.

But it was not easy. Dr. Light spoke a foreign language. He referred to something called "irrational guilt;" he said that certain thoughts were like a "loop;" and—worse—he wished for me to be "gentle" or "tender" with myself. Tender? Gentle? These sounded like the aphorisms on magnets you post on your refrigerator to perk you up. This generic peppy talk annoyed me. I had expected therapy to be like School where Dr. Light would help me by pointing out where I was wrong and telling me what I should do. But Dr. Light wouldn't play ball, declining to question my actions or instruct me to do anything. The harder I tried to blame myself and to get him to agree that I should be blamed, the more he resisted. Instead, he did something that nobody had done for me in School: he helped me.

The early days of therapy, however, required triage: I needed to get the suicidal ideations to stop as quickly as possible. It didn't happen overnight. I was prescribed medication, which helped, but the underlying trauma caused by School needed to be addressed head-on so that I could start to think straight. One of the earliest illuminations occurred in a session about my hopelessness with starting over, a topic we examined for several months.

One day, I was trying to explain to him that my law career could not be rebooted because I no longer had the emotional support of School and that a client like Podonok was hard to come by because the kind of work he gave me was usually done by big law firms. Plus, Podonok had hired me because of my connection to School.

I explained, "It was a unique situation, I was very lucky to have gotten to work for him. Think about Simon and Garfunkel. Simon played the guitar, wrote the songs. Garfunkel was great but all he did was sing. When they split up, Garfunkel couldn't play guitar or write songs, but Simon could. That's kind of like my situation: He can still make money in his business, write the songs, and play guitar, but I'm like Garfunkel. I was just a lucky sidekick."

Dr. Light thought for a moment. He asked, "So are you saying that you were lucky to be 'singing' with Podonok and that he's like Simon, of that stature?"

"Exactly."

"But isn't Podonok in trouble with the AG? Isn't he still involved with Sharon and heavily entrenched in School?"

I nodded my head.

Dr. Light continued, "And didn't Simon have his share of flops, never sell as many concert tickets as he did when he was with Garfunkel?"

I pushed back, "That is all true, but Simon can always get it back: he can put out a new album. He was the star of the duo."

"But can't you put out a new album?"

"I don't have the same star power as Podonok. Maybe I'll sell a few copies at most."

Dr. Light paused and said to me with a smile, "This sounds like you're talking about the 'Garfunkel Paradox.'"

I laughed. "What the hell is that?"

"Well, what do you think it is?"

"I would guess the Garfunkel Paradox is where you have to start a solo career after a successful career with a more talented partner."

Dr. Light shook his head, "The Garfunkel Paradox is the irrational belief that your best days are behind you when in fact it's the opposite. There is no truth to the claim that Garfunkel became a flop after the group split, nor that he was a lucky talentless sidekick. That is not how either of them saw it. Simon considered Garfunkel the superior singer. Garfunkel was 50 percent responsible for the brilliance that was the duo. After they broke up Garfunkel had a successful and fulfilling career—different, rocky at times, but apparently quite satisfying."

I had not thought about it that way; this made sense.

Dr. Light continued, "The Garfunkel Paradox is a false notion. It's not reality. There is no reason to think that your best days are behind you. In fact, it sounds to me like you were indispensable to the success of Podonok and that you have a lot to look forward to now that you're free from him and Sharon. Also, don't forget that School (and Podonok) reinforced this false narrative—this illusion—that without School (and Podonok) you are nothing."

Over many months and many conversations like this one, Dr. Light helped me to see the Garfunkel Paradox. He also helped me to give up the belief that money is an existential matter. I came to see that School's system was based upon the impossible demand that one could become perfect, and that perfectionism was making me miserable.

Dr. Light also helped me to see that my successes (for example, building my business) which I credited to School (and which School took credit for) were my own doing. It became clear to me that my father—who built his own business from scratch—had been my role model and that he had provided guidance and inspiration to me by example.

The process was slow, because Dr. Light and I had to discover the underlying causes and traumas that were buried away in a secret life I never discussed with anyone except people in School. One of these traumas occurred well before I was in School, having been only worsened by Sharon.

A few years after getting divorced, I met Yasmine. I was using the stationary bike at the McBurney YMCA. A woman breezed right past my bike to go on the track. She was wearing a spicy perfume. She was fast and I could not take my eyes off her. I introduced myself to her in the weight room. She smiled and shook my hand. "I'm Yasmine," she said in a French accent, "nice to meet you." Yasmine's eyes were dark, her cheekbones high, and she knew she was gorgeous and that I was making a total fool of myself. There was no good reason for her to agree to give me her phone number, but she did. She also agreed to get together, and we soon formed a tight, loving bond.

I sat in the swivel chair. Buddha was there. The tissues. Dr. Light. He was patient, waiting for me to speak.

I said, "A therapist that Sharon sent us to told me that the reason Beth and I stopped having sex was that I was gay."

Dr. Light showed surprise. In the year I'd been seeing him this had not come up. Also, he was aware that I was dating Yasmine, as well as other women, and I had never indicated an attraction to men.

"Oh, OK, why did he say this?" Dr. Light asked.

I explained the circumstances. And I told him about Maury.

He asked how it was that I felt responsible for having touched Maury. I told him I hadn't been forced—maybe mentally forced— but not physically forced. He asked, looking back, what I thought I could have done. I said I could have left the apartment. He asked whether I considered that it was 3:00 a.m. on the Lower East Side in the middle of winter and that I had nowhere to go and that I was fourteen. I told him that it didn't matter. He challenged me. He was getting me annoyed. It seemed like he was trying to talk me out of what I knew. It seemed like he was trying to talk me into not taking responsibility for my life. It sounded like he was just trying to cheer me up. I explained then that School was clear in teaching that there was something called "response to request" and that somehow I had requested Maury to force me to touch him. He asked me how I "requested" this, and I explained that I really owed it to Maury given all the fun times he'd showed me. Dr. Light wasn't getting anywhere. I told him that I thought he was just trying to make me feel better, and wasn't listening to what I did. This conversation lasted over the course of several months.

At some point, however, Dr. Light tried a new approach. He asked me, "Are there laws against having sex with persons under a certain age?"

"Yes, it's called statutory rape," I said.

"And isn't there something called age of consent?"

"Yeah, you're right, the age of consent in New York is seventeen. Sex with a person under the age of seventeen is statutory rape."[31]

"And why does the law exist?"

"Basically, the concept is that below a certain age, people—children—don't have the capacity to consent. They are presumed to be too young to be able to agree to have sex with someone older."

Dr. Light nodded. "So can you repeat what you just said?"

"You mean, children don't have the capacity to consent?"

Dr. Light nodded.

I considered this perspective and responded, "So you're saying, that I didn't have the capacity to consent even though I did it?"

Dr. Light just shrugged as if to say, yes, you just solved 5+6=11. He was patient, understanding, and he let me come to this myself, even though I had to count out the numbers on my fingers. He didn't even vocalize, "You're right." The "Dr. Light Shrug" allowed me to say it out loud without any prompting on the other side.

When I got home, I looked up the statutory rape laws and discovered that Maury had committed the misdemeanor of criminal sexual activity and the felony of facilitating a sex offense with a controlled

---

31 New York Penal Code § 130.05(3)(a).

substance.[32] He could have been locked up for several years. Probably more, because I remembered that several other campers had later told me that Maury had molested them, although they never called it that. But the most interesting thing I discovered is that under New York's Penal code, unlawful "sexual contact" outlaws "the touching of the actor by the victim."[33] This was new information: the definition of sex crimes includes a situation where the victim touches the defendant. In other words, the law understands that lack of consent can involve situations where the underage victim *touches the defendant*. If the criminal law cannot blame me, then I cannot blame me. When I related this to Dr. Light, he just gave his shrug.

Then we talked about Sharon's theory that I was "experimenting." Dr. Light asked me to put a hypothetical fourteen year old boy in my place and ask myself whether that boy had been experimenting. No thinking required: I would feel he'd been sexually assaulted. Dr. Light also reminded me that Sharon and Dr. White talked about Beth and me, and that Sharon must have relayed her demented views to Dr. White, the quack. Finally, Dr. Light and I discussed that the foundation of my marriage to Beth was built on shaky ground and constantly under pressure and the influence of a cruel and manipulative woman. The gay narrative was a false one, started by the molester and perpetuated by Sharon, with an assist by Dr. White.

Now that the truth was out, however, it was hard for me not to judge myself for having gotten this wrong for so many years: for thinking something was wrong with me. Being hard on myself for being hard on myself was—and is—an endless loop of suffering. Around this time I saw *Spotlight*, the film about the investigative reporting done by the *Boston Globe* to uncover the scores of Catholic priests who abused boys. One victim, a grown man, talked about his abuse as a teenager. It rang so familiar: the guilt, shame, fear, and the silence. Dr. Light helped spell it out for me more clearly the next time we met: *it was not your fault that Maury molested you, and it was not your fault you blamed yourself.*

---

32 New York Penal Code § 130.90.

33 New York Penal Code § 130.00(3).

A couple of days later I saw Yasmine, we ordered in, she broke out some weed to smoke—I hadn't smoked any since my teens—and we sat on the big yellow couch in my living room. We started to kiss. She got up to go to the bathroom. I put on a live album by Dexter Gordon. The hard-bop song "Gingerbread Boy" played, probably a good choice for working out but not for mood music. But before I could change it, Yasmine returned and we started to make love. There was something about this moment, this combination of music, my emotional and physical connection with Yasmine, her tenderness, the weed, what Dr. Light had helped to reveal. The chorus of the song came back out of a piano solo, and I suddenly had a powerful realization about myself and my sexuality and the Maury lie and it all made sense to me and it was all confirmed in that instant. Yasmine and Dr. Light were the perfect pairing of experience and revelation.

Every toxin I was exposed to in School had to be purged; every lesson had to be unlearned; and every prejudice had to be exposed.

Some years after I escaped from School, I met Scott at the track at the McBurney YMCA. I had gotten back into running so I could cross-train with swimming. About my age, Scott was another runner, but a little slower than me. One day my regular running buddies didn't show so we ran together. Scott had a wide smile and was funny and smart. A former executive for CBS, he'd gone to Harvard and gotten his MBA from Columbia. One of the things about Scott that I immediately liked was that he listened to me without any kind of judgment. There were no conditions and no criticisms. I was still surprised by this when I made new friends. The conversations were fun, so we started to plan to meet for runs and quickly became workout buddies.

One day when we were running around the track, a man waved to Scott. Scott waved back. I asked him who it was. "Oh that's my husband, Kevin." When I said, "I didn't know you were gay," he answered something like, "I'm as gay as the day is long." About a month later I met his husband, Kevin, a surgeon and also an excellent

athlete. The three of us started running together, early mornings, for
an hour or more, on the High Line and on the West Side along the
Hudson River. We talked about everything: politics, current events,
the weather, aches and pains, other people out running, my involvement in School (a favorite topic of Scott's), love, life, and sex. Scott
and Kevin were "gold star gays," which means neither of them had
ever had sex with a woman. It was a term I'd never heard and a
concept which went against my understanding of homosexuality: I
had been trained to believe it was a choice one made. But Scott and
Kevin, particularly Scott, explained it to me without patronizing. "I
have only ever loved men. I didn't become gay. I *am* gay. I was born
gay. I didn't make a choice and it's definitely not a preference. It is
who I am." This was a revelation. It made sense. It also helped me to
frame my own questions. I became at ease with having gay men as
friends and not thinking that made me gay (a common hetero fear).
Scott joked that I am "friends of family," and it's true: the courage of
gay men and women to be out always inspires me because they are
not afraid of who they are. Who does not want to be who they are?
Who does not want to love who they want to love? Scott and Kevin
showed me this.

Angry, Evil Blogging

In addition to swimming and running, my new community of friends, and Dr. Light's therapy, I found solace, truth, and freedom in writing about School. There were several anonymous blogs out there about School but two that stood out: Esotericfreedom.com and The Gentle Souls Revolution (cultconfessions2.com). Written by former members of School, they were dedicated to pulling back the curtain on Sharon and telling their stories. They were also intended to help survivors. Esotericfreedom.com focused more on investigative matters: publishing information in the public record about Sharon and Alex. The Gentle Souls Revolution tended toward essays analyzing not only School's tactics but cults in general. They attracted many survivors of School who posted comments about their experiences. When I was in School, we were cautioned not to read the blogs written by "angry, evil former students." When Sharon somehow learned that a student named Jason was reading the blogs online, she blasted him in class, calling him a "cocksucking bastard." I was not alone in thinking that Sharon had some way to surveil our web usage.

But now I was free, and on January 1, 2016, I created a blog (cultrevolt.com) and published this post:

Not Another Damn Anonymous Blogger

I don't begrudge those evil-doer bloggers who prefer to remain anonymous. There are many good reasons to do so, especially for fear of retribution—real or imagined. But I prefer not to be anonymous. I want the world to know who I am. And what I went through. And to expose my opinion of Sharon to the world and to her followers, who are victims. If one or two can be enlightened to leave, that's great. If none, well . . . Sharon won't live forever, even though she thinks she is God.

I was a member of the Gans group for over 20 years. I didn't realize it was really a cult until I took the step, out the door. Ironically, that's when I finally felt and tasted the very freedom that had eluded me during my 20 years of "working on myself." In the topsy-turvy Gans world, lies are used to keep people in. She drills this into people to become fearful of leaving, to be fully dependent upon her, and to doubt oneself. It's kind of an invisible knot that she ties around her followers. She didn't invent this method of abuse, but she is very good at it. Sharon's motives are clear to every single former member, but completely hidden to anyone still there.

I hope you like the posts. I want people to leave the cult. To the extent I make factual claims, I endeavor to be accurate. If you think anything is inaccurate or is bothersome, don't hesitate to contact me here.

Happy New Year,
Spencer

In the early months, I posted almost every day. And yeah, it was cathartic for me. I didn't want to admit that because that wasn't the only reason I was posting. I was posting because I wanted justice. I wanted to do the one thing that I could do to bring justice: to speak out and to expose them. And so I did. Here is one of the earliest posts, called "To Sharon (With Sorrow)":

It's really the most shameful joke of them all. That Sharon describes herself as a teacher. Let's identify some of Sharon's treachery, manipulation, and "class-room" antics.

And then let's see how we'd would feel if our child (including a college age child) had a teacher who did any of these things:

1. Insulted or humiliated a child in a classroom full of students.

2. Yelled at a child for no apparent reason and demanded penance.

3. Made fun of a child.

4. Came into class drunk.

5. Came into class late. Missed classes for no reason. Erratic attendance.

6. Came into class and crapped out on a La-Z-Boy in full repose.

7. Slept during class.

8. Kept the class going until she decided to go home. Babbling on and on. Incoherent at times.

9. Got involved in a child's personal life such as suggesting who the child should be friends with, suggesting that the child no longer speak with her parents, and tell people what she really thought of them. Imagine if you asked your child how her day was, and she had been instructed to say, "none of your goddamn business."

10. Blew hot and cold. One day a child is head of the class, next day she is verbally assaulted.

11. Encouraged the students to bad-mouth each other and snitch on them.

12. Was in love with herself.

13. Called a girl student a "cunt" and told her to "just get over" her mother's suicide "already."

14. Claimed she was responsible for the election of Obama.

15. Insisted all the students unanimously praise her, no matter what.

16. Would not suffer gladly anyone who challenged her in the slightest.

17. Had no idea what she was saying. Rambled. Spoke of her brilliance. Complained about how the world was unfair to her. Lamented that she could have been a film starlet. Claimed she had sex with Frank Sinatra, was close friends with the Beatles, and bragged she was on a first-name basis with many famous actor/people from 1970s and on– Bob, Meryl, Dustin, Paul, Liza, Andy . . .

18. Had only passing superficial familiarity with the subject matter which she rarely ever discussed, instead focusing on a child's pressing personal problems, such as who they are dating, their home life, and their religion.

19. Had never studied the subject. Had gone straight to teaching. Never certified.

20. Was openly bigoted against people of color and homosexuals.

21. Constantly complained about her health and exhibited hypochondria.

22. Was a liar and sociopath.

23. Insisted on being paid in cash or check to a mysterious LLC.

24. All students failed and were left back over and over and over.

25. Discussed in class her sex life with her husband and other lovers in graphic, embarrassing detail.

26. Suggested that she had sex with a student teacher—we could be "friends that fuck."

27. Would randomly throw students out of class.

28. Had children wait on her hand and foot.

29. Gave detailed sex advice to students in front of the entire class.

30. Constantly sought pity.

31. Lived in the Plaza Hotel.

32. Forced students to work on personal building projects in unsafe conditions and for free.

33. Forced students to cook her all her meals.
34. Showed favoritism to some students (usually the wealth-iest).
35. Sought and received financial support to support her extravagant lifestyle.

This teacher would be fired, arrested, jailed, and become internationally known as a "devil."

So if no parent would entrust their child to such a devil, why should any rational person attend a single class with this evil person?

Please let me know of any other characteristics and I will add to the list . . .

Love, SS

And so began a several-year project which continues. I have been able to get at least a few people out of School who happened upon my blog. I kept in touch with other survivors. I have heard from relatives of members. I learned how to write about the cult. And I vented my anger and expressed my sorrow and other feelings. And a lot of people read it and comment. I befriended the brilliant author of the blog "Gentle Souls Revolution," Esther Friedman, who has done so much work in the field of cults; she is a treasured, supportive friend.

The Gans Racket:
Crime, Power, and Depravity

Other than saying in class once that she became a teacher because someone told her she would make a "great" one and that her Aim was to become a "lover," Sharon never discussed her motivations. A lover of what she did not say, but I take her at her word: Sharon loved nothing more than power. Everything she did revolved around her obtaining power. She wanted power over people and all facets of their lives, she wanted to have people's full attention and devotion, and she wanted people's money. She wanted a complete proxy to control everyone's life and with that proxy she took whatever she wanted. She got off on it. And the ends justified the means. When I went to Montana I saw that School was big business and that she was making a lot of money, in cash. It was a family business, started by a pair of lunatics—Alex and Sharon. They monetized their ability to spot people's vulnerabilities. They took advantage of people who were hungry for meaning, inquisitive, and living in challenging times. They understood well that living and working in Manhattan and Boston isn't easy and it's enticing to give up one's agency to somebody who purports to offer community and who tells you what to do. And they were able to recruit members who were willing to be their accomplices.

Other than that time she announced that she and Fred were "friends who fuck," I saw no evidence that Sharon was sleeping with anyone else in School, although our date night was unnerving. But sex was always on Sharon's mind, and she got sexual gratification in many ways. I understand that her husband Alex Horn (who stopped teaching before I got involved in School) was a sexual predator. There are rumors that he raped at least one woman, and I believe it. I saw with my own eyes that Alex was a violent sociopath. He was obsessed with proving his masculinity and making others prove theirs. He picked fights and he instigated ones. He liked to beat up his students (because they didn't fight back), and he liked to see other people get into physical fights, encouraging men to coldcock unsuspecting others. One of these episodes landed a man in the hospital with a wired jaw who ended up coming back to class and apologizing to his attacker for "being asleep." I'm told that Alex once instructed Robert Klein to coldcock someone for no reason. Alex got off on watching people fight. Same with Sharon; recall the boxing match at Gleason's. One other thing: a few former members have told me that Sharon actively recruited certain women to be Alex's concubines, because she couldn't stop him, but wanted to control who he slept with.

Sharon and Alex claimed there were three levels of sex, in "descending order." The first is "suprasexuality" where sex is used to "perfect the soul." Sharon claimed Christ, Buddha, and others were suprasexual. The next level is normal sexuality, which is sex for pro-creation. The last category is called "infra-sex" which involves the "misuse of the sexual organs or sexual energy." This includes Ouspensky's list of perversions: "pornography, prostitution, masturbation, homosexuality, and asexuality." Sex for gratification is also a perversion, according to Ouspensky. Therefore, unless people are having sex for procreation or perfecting a soul, it is always infra-sex. Sharon and Alex contended that they had suprasex. And, of course, they also contended that there was no such thing as adultery and they openly and routinely encouraged married couples to have sex outside their marriage. They were advocates of polyamory.

Several women told me (after I left School) that Fred and at least one other male teacher had sexually assaulted them. There was another teacher who broke up a marriage so he could marry the wife. The power dynamics were severe in School because we were conditioned to never challenge teachers. I know that former members are understandably fearful and ashamed of speaking out about anything involving School, but I hope that my story will encourage them to come out and confront their predators. Mind you, none of this happened without Sharon's knowledge and consent.

I didn't have firsthand knowledge of any sexual or physical assaults while I was in School, but I realized that there was something fishy going on in terms of financial improprieties.

At first I didn't think much about the cash tuition payments. There were only sixty or so people in my class and I figured it just went to pay the rent for the loft we used. But when I later realized that there were hundreds of students, and when I did the math, I realized that Sharon was grossing over a million dollars a year, in cash. And that meant only one thing: she probably wasn't reporting it. At some point, however, Sharon decided that some students should pay in checks but others in cash and I learned after I left School that School kept two sets of books, reporting only the income earned from checks. Later I found out about brown paper bags filled with tens of thousands of dollars which were shuttled to Sharon by trusted couriers. I also learned about their elaborate schemes of tax evasion, money laundering, charity fraud, and other financial crimes.

Sometime in the late 1990s, Sharon decided that School should have a property in upstate New York for monthly retreats—she called it "CR," short for country retreats. It would be like Montana, but more people would attend, and she would come and speak and of course receive extra tuition payments. An elaborate plan was hatched to create a phony charitable corporation called Artists in the Country or ATC. This allowed Sharon to collect donations from students, which the students could deduct as charitable contributions and which Sharon wouldn't have to pay taxes on. ATC collected over a $1 million from students, some of whom gave six figures. People gave inheritances, others cleared out retirement accounts, savings accounts. A large amount was donated by a scion of a cosmetics company family who was a longtime member. A property was located, and it was built out over the course of a year with several structures, including a house for Sharon. The construction

was performed day and night by members of School who paid Sharon for the "privilege" of working; it was grueling and dangerous
work and I worked there for several months, painting, hammering,
digging, pouring cement, chainsawing trees, and the rest of it. But
Sharon had another issue: property taxes. She didn't want to pay
them. So, they sought a property tax exemption from the town on
the grounds that this was an artists' foundation. She claimed that
the foundation sponsored a dozen artists of different disciplines to
study and perform there each summer. Brochures were created, ads
taken out, performances given, wining and dining of the town offi-
cials, and even more. But this was a complete fabrication. There was
no intention to ever hold an artists' colony there. It was a weekend
getaway for Sharon's cult, and it was completely for her profit. The
town rejected the tax waiver—not because they thought that ATC
was a fraud but because they believed that an artists' colony did not
merit a property tax waiver under state law. Sharon directed that
a lawsuit be brought in the name of ATC against the town. Mind
you, however, that Sharon's name was nowhere to be seen in any
of this. She was not on the board of ATC or on any of the papers.
ATC officers were all members of School. After the suit was filed,
it became clear to Sharon and the others that things were going
poorly. Shortly after that, two members of ATC—students of School
whom I knew well—asked me to meet them for lunch in midtown.
Both men went to Ivy League colleges and were highly successful in
the financial industry. It was a dark restaurant in a fancy hotel, and
we were seated in the back. I thought I was in the *Godfather: Part II.*
They started to explain to me that the ATC was in fact a fabrication.
I told them that they had to drop the lawsuit and sell the property
and return the money to charity. One of them, Carl, asked me what
would happen if they pushed the case. I told him he would probably
end up in jail. He said, "This is the Work, and this is worth going to
jail for." This was not the first time a member of School said something like this to me. A teacher once told me that he would gladly
kill for Sharon if asked, so I wasn't surprised when Carl said this. I
just thought it was ridiculous to believe that it is morally correct to
commit tax fraud and I said so. The lunch ended. I never discussed

this again, but a couple of months later I learned that they dropped the case, sold the property, gave the money to charity, and dissolved ATC.

Construction projects were not confined to upstate and Montana. There were dozens of construction projects where members were coerced into working in dangerous conditions for free. Sharon's and Alex's apartments were built with forced labor; the spaces where we met to hold meetings were built with forced labor; Sharon's home in the Hamptons was renovated with forced labor; Sharon coerced students to renovate homes of her favored students. As with all the other construction labor, we were paying for the privilege of being forced to build for Sharon and others. The projects always involved impossible deadlines set arbitrarily by Sharon or other leaders. I recall the gut renovation of School's former space in Chelsea, on West Twenty-fifth Street, where we worked through the night for months during a summer in the late 2000s. I'll never forget the sight of sixty-five-year-old Joni, with her chronic illnesses, standing on a ten-foot ladder at 2:30 a.m. with a paint roller in her hand, furiously painting the ceiling to meet a 3:00 a.m. deadline.

After I escaped School, I decided to find out as much as I could about Sharon and School. I gathered information from the public record and I spoke to former students, including many I never knew while in School. I wanted to find out how Sharon handled the millions of dollars of cash she collected. A former student from the Boston group, Murray, told me of one method used more than thirty years ago. Murray was known by Sharon to be wealthy. Fred told Murray that School needed his "help." Murray agreed. It was arranged for him to meet Fred in the underground parking lot of Murray's bank. Fred handed him $100,000 in cash which Murray then put in his safe deposit box. Murray then wrote a check for $100,000 to the order of a corporation which was controlled by Sharon. Murray was then given a promissory note from the corporation which agreed to "repay" this "loan." Of course, this was not a loan. To further cover their tracks, Murray agreed to list interest income on his personal taxes from this "loan." There was no interest income. School, however, did reimburse him for the taxes he paid for this income. I'm not aware of any other instances of this scheme but I find it hard to believe that it was isolated given the millions Sharon pulled in over the years.

Sharon had many homes and properties—in the Hamptons, Montana, Westchester, Mexico, and Manhattan—all of which were used exclusively by Sharon and her family. None, however, were in her name. Her home in the Plaza Hotel was purchased in about 2007 for over $8 million by a limited liability company. I saw the apartment on two occasions. It faced the park and was deluxe, fit for a queen. When we drove up to the building the first time, Sharon casually told me, "Oh, Alex and I always wanted to live in the Plaza," as though it was a mere bucket list item like skydiving or seeing the running of the bulls in Pamplona.

At best, Sharon had a passing knowledge of the Gurdjieff system. She rarely lectured on any of the Fourth Way literature, largely confining her remarks, classes, and meetings to dispensing advice with occasional references to Fourth Way terminology. It was an unspoken assumption among students that Sharon only wanted to discuss people's personal lives and not the Fourth Way. After I left School, I learned from another survivor that Sharon repeated things she heard on Oprah as if they were her own ideas. Once during class, a student excitedly remarked that she had heard Sharon's exact bit of wisdom expressed on Oprah that very day. Sharon said nothing, shooting daggers back to the woman.[34]

Other than getting paid by people to ruin their lives, Sharon held no job or occupation. She did, however, directly receive regular profits from at least one business owned by a member of School and possibly from others. Sharon was the beneficiary of all kinds of valuable "gifts" from her students throughout her life. These included foreign cars, the use of private jets, a classic Chris-Craft boat, a custom-fitted Winnebago, jewelry, a hot tub, artwork, high-end electronics, furniture, rugs, clothing, and first-class airfare. And then there were

---

34 We were forbidden to read any biographies about Gurdjieff. Several biographies paint him as a charlatan who defrauded and mercilessly abused his followers, and claim that his "system" was plagiarized piecemeal from legitimate sources, resulting in an inscrutable, incoherent mess.

all the coerced student services we provided to Sharon, including maid services, medical care, all meals and snacks prepared by members (including me), accounting and bookkeeping, personal security, chauffeur (I was one of them), massages, errands, shopping, wake-up service, and round-the-clock care for Sharon and family (me again). All of this was in addition to the free labor provided for construction projects, maintenance, gardening, and anything else Sharon could possibly imagine. This chart below illustrates.

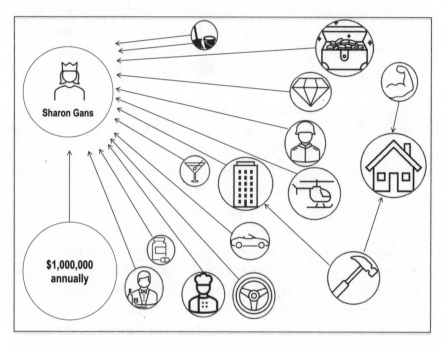

Sharon did not consider anything about her followers as off-limits, including aspects of her follower's children's lives: from conception to how and where children were raised.

Of all of her crimes and immorality, Sharon outdid herself when it came to children. Her depravity knew no limits. There is no greater act of sadism than to harm families and children and Sharon loved it. Her casual urging that I have sex with my wife's teenage daughter was one instance. She broke up families willy-nilly, devised onerous custody situations, and kept parents out of the house several nights a week going to class, doing recruiting, doing chores for her, or preparing for parties in her honor. Still, many of her followers actively sought—and took—her advice in this area for a variety of reasons—fear, ignorance, to show loyalty, and because they had no conscience, not an ounce. It should be said that even if she wanted to give good advice, Sharon was uniquely unqualified in this area. Sharon claimed that children loved her because she was always in her Essence, but I never once saw a child not frightened of her.

Sharon and Alex wanted their followers to stay close and encouraged intra-School marriages and for couples to have as many children as possible. This is standard in all kinds of cults and closed communities. Even if one parent leaves, the children are essentially held hostage, and this scenario has kept many people from speaking out about School.

I know of at least half a dozen private adoptions which Sharon arranged, almost all of them between members of School. I'm aware of one situation where she arranged for a child to be taken from an unmarried couple because she claimed that they would be terrible parents and the child would probably die of neglect. Sharon was opposed to abortions in all cases, saying it was murder. When adoptions occurred, she directed the parents not to tell the children that they were adopted. In one case, an adopted child, then in her thirties, was contacted by her biological mother (another student) and informed of the truth. It was also not uncommon for single mothers of small children to get married to male members who then pretended to be the biological fathers. Sharon had asked me to do this with another woman before I got married to Beth, but I was not interested in the woman or this crazy lie.

Except for infants, children did not attend classes, and the only time they would see Sharon was on Retreat in Montana. Children did not attend Retreat meetings or do any work—they played and had a great time. But this was a special time for Sharon, because she got to see the children firsthand and criticize them and us. She told one couple that their nine-year old daughter was destined to be giving "blow jobs to thirteen-year-old boys" judging by the girl's bad manners. She told another couple that they were the worst parents because they allowed their son to call them by their first names (which is kind of funny because her children called her Sharon.) Sharon instructed parents to forbid their children from watching television, having cell phones, or using any social media. These instructions were followed by many, including the parents of the girl with the bad manners. When Sharon learned that the girl had never even seen a movie in a theater, she ridiculed the parents for lacking "common sense." On several occasions, Sharon instructed parents to keep a framed photo of themselves on prominent display in their homes in order to message to the children that the parents' marriage was "more important than the children."

Survivors

I knew Bruce would be caught off guard to hear from me out of nowhere. Twenty-four years earlier he was the one calling me. "Hey, remember me?"

He hesitated for a second. "Oh my God. Spencer? How are you?"

"I'm finally out," I said. This was obvious since I wouldn't have called him if I weren't.

"I'm so glad. When?"

"I left three months ago. Let's have a drink and I'll fill you in," I said.

A couple of nights later I was waiting for Bruce at a neighborhood BBQ place on East Eighteenth between Park Avenue and Irving Place. Bruce looked the same: handsome, thick black hair, preppy clothes, like he'd walked right out of an Abercrombie & Fitch ad. We hugged and ordered drinks. I filled him in.

He said he was now retired and happily married. It struck me that this was the first time we were together that it was unpressured, unmonitored, and not false. There were no agendas and no requirements. There was no script. We had each had our own awful experience, an awful trauma, and managed to survive. I did, however, have some unfinished business.

I told Bruce that I wished he hadn't pursued me, hadn't invited me to join School. He could tell I was asking for an apology. I needed to hear it.

Bruce looked at me carefully and was gracious and willing to give me what I really needed. He said in a soft but sincere voice, "Spencer, I'm terribly sorry about that. I do mean that."

I thanked him and I told him he was forgiven. But I also acknowledged that I understood that he meant no harm or wrongdoing—to the contrary, he was inviting me to something he truly loved. He was a victim as much as me. I told him I knew he would never mean harm. It was a delicate moment, but Bruce is a decent man who had been through as much hell as I had been, if not more. It was the first time that there was any truth in our relationship. We wished each other well and parted.

My next call was to Jimmy, at his business. He accused me of being a spy for his mother and did not believe I had left School. We spent the next forty-five minutes arguing about whether his accusation was true. I was unable to convince him and frankly I didn't blame him. He had been raised by a demented mother and must have suffered more than anyone under her tyranny. But six months later he reached out to me and invited me to his home. Jimmy was quite clear in his mind that School was a cult and had not spoken to his mother for well over a decade. He had completely abandoned School and all the Work ideas. He was happy and productive and pursuing his own life.

Other survivors were not, however, in sync with my experience.

My old friend Russell, who was booted from School because he could not rearrange his schedule to go to Montana, challenged me. "You sound angry, and I think that is clouding your judgment. The Work looks at anger as a negative emotion," he counseled me. Russell also informed me he was still studying the Fourth Way and was grateful to Sharon for kicking him out because "my valuation was not strong enough."

Molly left School several years before me. She was happy to hear from me and we spent some time together. Molly had kept in touch with several other survivors we both had known. She said she was hosting regular get-togethers where they would discuss books and spiritual matters. Molly suggested that I read a book about forgiveness and that I "should start to forgive Sharon." She also invited me to one of her meetings, which I declined. I got the feeling she was going to tell me what to do and I had been there and done that.

After these calls with Russell and Molly, Dr. Light and I discussed anger and the advice that I should forgive Sharon. Dr. Light was surprised to hear that I shouldn't be angry at anyone, especially Sharon, or that I should forgive anyone for anything, especially Sharon. His message had always been for me to make my own decisions as to what I want to do in my life and how I think and feel, something I had to relearn. Dr. Light liked to use legal analogies. "Correct me if I'm wrong—because I'm talking about your area of expertise—but isn't there some concept in the law about the principal witness to an event being the most reliable witness?" he asked. "Wouldn't it be fair to say that when it comes to your own impressions, sense of reality, emotions, sense of rightness, and life choices that you are the principal witness? In other words, that you know better than anyone about yourself?" he asked. Dr. Light and I came to use the phrase *the principal witness* as referring to self-determination. This concept has helped me to survive the decades of gaslighting and to recognize when it's going on.

Over the years I have spoken to dozens of survivors, most of whom I knew while we were in School. Each survivor has had a different experience—some still like to read the Fourth Way books. A handful of survivors, like my dear friend Jane Roth, are certain, after close study of the group and the Fourth Way's history, that School is a cult. I believe all of them have scars and suffered some level of trauma. But without exception, all of the ones I have met are happier now that they have self-determination. I've seen that people digest their experiences differently. And with most there's a mutual understanding that we will not tell each other what to do.

After I left, I tried to contact a few of the members in School but only one was willing to speak with me: a fellow named Billy. I tried to tell him it was a dangerous place, but he wouldn't listen to me and eventually blocked my calls.

Several months after I left School, I was standing in front of the pastry case at Veniero's on East Eleventh Street on a late August afternoon when I saw "Unknown" was calling me. I knew that would be someone involved in School because they always blocked their numbers. I answered.

"Oh, I'm glad I got you," Sharon sang in her falsetto.

The adrenaline surged and I gathered my wits. "Hi, Sharon. How nice to hear from you," I lied. It was the first time I ever felt more powerful than Sharon.

"Oh, well you left so suddenly that we didn't get a chance to say goodbye so I'm calling now to send my regards to you and to see how you are."

To see how I am? She was ridiculously transparent. So, I called her out. "Well, you know how I am from talking to Beth."

She lied again. "I never talk to Beth about you."

"I'm doing better than ever, Sharon, how about you?"

Then she went on for ten minutes straight about how her daughter was suffering from cancer caused by the negativity of her divorce and her brother Jimmy. I listened, thinking what a pathetic and deranged person she was, how classically narcissistic it was to try to gain sympathy to deflect from her own cruelty. After her pity speech I told her I had to take another call and got off. We never spoke again.

Shortly after that, I heard that Sharon had announced one night in class that I was gay, that she had tried to help me "straighten out," and that's why my marriage failed.

In June 2015, Fred Mindel had a heart attack and died at age seventy. His obituary said that he had "inspired others to lead fulfilling and meaningful lives."

A few years later Sharon had a falling-out with Robert Klein and kicked him out of School for unknown reasons.

In January 2021, Sharon died of COVID-19, alone, in her home in the Plaza Hotel at the age of eighty-five. I understand she had declined to be hospitalized and denied that she even had COVID-19.

As of this writing, School continues to meet. Sharon's will bequeathed her interest in the legal entity which runs School to four leaders of School so they can perpetuate the mission.

The long arm of Sharon Gans reaches beyond the grave, covering the mouths of current and former victims. It's no different than the pedophile priests or coaches who can keep their victims quiet. Survivors suffer shame, embarrassment, self-blame, and a perceived stigmatization of having been duped by a cult. I have found nothing but understanding and empathy from family, friends, clients, and strangers alike.

The graves of Sharon Gans (left) and Alex Horn, located at Shaarey Pardes Cemetery, Old Stone Highway, Springs, New York. Courtesy of the author.

Straight Down the Hudson

On a steamy August morning in 2016, five of us jumped into the Hudson River off a small boat fifty yards south of the Battery on the tip of Manhattan. We wore nothing but goggles, swimsuits, caps, and sunscreen. The water was seventy-one degrees and flat.

We were about to commence an approximately eight-hour swim, counterclockwise, around Manhattan. We would head north in the East River, cut west to the Harlem River, go northward till it spills under the Spuyten Duyvil Bridge (which connects the Bronx and Manhattan), and then go left to head south down the Hudson River, passing under the George Washington Bridge, and back to the starting line at the Battery. About twenty-eight miles give or take. We would swim under the twenty bridges connecting three boroughs and New Jersey to Manhattan. This swim was the culmination of a few years of training and miles and hours of open water swimming.

We got the go-ahead and we were off. When embarking on a marathon swim, one mustn't think too far ahead—it's overwhelming. It's best not to think much beyond the next thirty minutes, which is when you get to stop for a drink and snack.

Within minutes my mind drifted off into "swimming zone." My senses filled—the murky seaweed-green water; my kayaker Pat; the Manhattan and Brooklyn skylines—those tall buildings taller from the perspective of being prone in the river; the sound of my breathing; the swooshing of the water; foggy goggles strapped over my face; the surprisingly pleasant taste of the East River that I would describe as salty with a nose of barnacle. I looked ahead and saw the other swimmers two hundred yards ahead of me. I sprinted and caught up with them as we all swam under the Brooklyn Bridge.

Back into swimming zone, my thoughts turned to the last words of the race organizer before we splashed in: "You will need to swim quickly up until Ninety-sixth Street so that we can keep the tide with us." But it's hard to judge swim pace, especially on a multi-hour swim. I felt strong, and did a quick inventory: hips rotating? check; kicking consistently? check; head position correct? check; stroke smooth and steady? check; bending my elbow in the water with arms shoulder distance apart? check; strong pulls—making each one count? not at all. "Damn, I hate when that happens. Why can't I remember to do that?" But then I reminded myself to be gentle on myself and that this was not a test and that I had nothing to prove.

The piano intro to Billy Joel's "Summer, Highlands Falls" played in my head. I always latch onto a tune to help me keep a rhythm and keep me occupied for the stretches. Billy Joel said the song is about manic depression, with the left hand playing the depression part, and the right hand playing the manic part.

I saw Aaron, my main crewman—and one of the world's best— signaling me from the pilot boat that it was time to stop for a feed—i.e., for water and calories. My friend Ken was assisting him.

Successfully swimming such a distance without a great crew is impossible because of the hazards and helplessness of being in the open water, especially one of the world's busiest waterways. Each of the five swimmers had been assigned a kayaker and a thirty-foot powered-pilot boat that guides the kayaker and protects us from larger boats. There are several people on the pilot boat: an official observer who is like a referee making sure swimmers comply with the rules; a main crewperson who is responsible for the swimmers' well-being; and possibly an assistant crewperson.

We made sixteen stops in our circle around Manhattan, and each time Aaron told me my stroke count, where we were, how far I had swum since the last stop, and something upbeat and encouraging ("your kick looks great"). One of the rules was that I couldn't hold on to the boat, let alone even touch it during the stops, and so I would tread water during the feeds. Aaron's positive tone was calming. I looked forward to each feed for these pep talks. My entire crew was cheerful and optimistic, including the observer, Martina, who photographed me throughout the eight-hour swim.

I went into some dark places in my head during the swim: "I'm not going to finish this. My arms are killing me. I'm so hungry. I don't seem to be moving. The water is hot. I'm tired. I want my bed." I went back to Billy Joel. I thought about my son and how I didn't want to have to tell him that I quit. I decided I would finish no matter what. At the next feed, just north of the George Washington Bridge, Aaron told me that our pace was faster than average: "It's just a straight shot down the Hudson. Just keep swimming, Spencer, you got this."

I passed Chelsea Piers at West Twenty-third Street to my left. My mind went to School. I thought about their hypocrisy, lies, abuse, hatred, and crimes. I thought about how swimming had been the key to my survival. And then I did an inventory. Make each stroke count. And then I switched mental stations back to Billy Joel's song, fueled by his piano lick, full circle to the base of Manhattan where I had started eight hours before.

Swimming straight down the Hudson River, circling Manhattan.
Courtesy of Martina Pavlicova.

Acknowledgments

The entire team at Skyhorse Publishing and Arcade have been wonderful to work with. Tony Lyons believed in the value of sharing this story to a wide audience; Mark Gompertz gave invaluable feedback and support; Lilly Golden expertly and patiently turned my manuscript into a final product—I was lucky to work with her.

I am grateful to David Rattray and Bess Rattray, publishers, respectively, of *The East Hampton Star* and *East Magazine* for publishing my article about School in July 2019. I am indebted to Cornelia Channing for editing that article and teaching me how not to write like a lawyer.

Friends and colleagues encouraged me to write, finish, and publish this book: Stacey Sosa for all her "connections;" Anabel Sosa for the title and constant support; Kimberly for planting the seeds; Andy Ostroy for convincing me this is a story worth telling; Michael DeCapite for telling me to keep writing and stop editing; David Falk and Vicki Birdoff for kindness and love; Eric Rayman, Esq., for expert counsel and strategy; Kevin and Julie Trainor for being there, literally; Candy Renee, Yasmine, and Deborah (at Tower Five); and Phyllis Ho, Kenn Lichtenwalter, Bonnie Schwartz Nolan, Caite Kappel, Dan Medeiros, Greg Williams, Jeremy Grosvenor, Evan Drutman, Elke Hofmann, Arnie Toren, Fran Alioto, Sharon Oliensis, Jane Roth, Esther Friedman, Stephanie Rosenberg, and Shara Frederick for being my sounding boards.

This book would not have been possible without Pamela Meyer and Mitch Gordon.

And finally, I am forever indebted to my oldest friends and family for helping me get my life back: Sue and Owen Perla, Maria Deutscher and Joel Siegel, Jennifer Carter and Colin Campbell, and Melissa and Matthew Schneider. My mother has reliably dispensed good advice, helped me find just the right words, and has always been funny. My son deserves special thanks for his perfect love, sweetness, and wisdom.

Appendix

There are many excellent books, articles, and websites about cults which can be readily discovered on any search engine. Here are my favorites: Amanda Montell's *Cultish: The Language of Fanaticism*; Rick Ross's *Cults Inside Out: How People Get In and Can Get Out*; and Margaret Thaler Singer's *Cults in Our Midst: The Continuing Fight Against Their Hidden Menace*.

Here are several recommended websites about cults in general as well as School: culteducation.com; cultconfessions2.com; icsahome. com; freedomofmind.com; cultrevolt.com.

There are several books about cults, traumas, and challenging lives that helped me understand my experiences. In no particular order: Faith Jones's *Sex Cult Nun;* Emma Cline's *The Girls*; Deborah Feldman's *Unorthodox: The Scandalous Rejection of My Hasidic Roots*; Kathryn Harrison's *The Kiss*; Leah Remini's *Troublemaker: Surviving Hollywood and Scientology*; Jeannette Walls's *The Glass Castle*; Shawna Kay Rodenberg's *Kin*; Carolyn Jessop's *Escape*; Sarah Edmondson's *Scarred*; and J. R. Moehringer's *The Tender Bar.*

I recommend three classic books about confronting trauma: Jon Kabat-Zinn's *Full Catastrophe Living: Using the Wisdom of Your Body and Mind to Face Stress, Pain, and Illness;* Viktor Frankl's *Man's Search for Meaning;* and Edith Eva Eger's *The Choice: Embrace the Possible.*

Nine Telltale Signs You're in a Cult

1. You give an inordinate amount of time and money to the group.

2. The group's ideology is strict, exacting, and unforgiving.

3. Your life is highly regulated by the group.

4. You cannot challenge the leaders or the ideology—their word is final.

5. The leaders will punish you for breaking the rules of the group.

6. Former members are ostracized and denigrated.

7. The group isolates you from your friends and family.

8. The group discourages you from thinking for yourself.

9. You are afraid to leave the group.

About the Author

Spencer Schneider is a native of Long Island and practices law. After his escape from School, Mr. Schneider took up marathon and winter swimming, became an ocean lifeguard, and started the blog about School called "Cult Revolt." A contributing writer for *East Magazine*, he lives in New York.